Scientific Boxing and Self Defence

Scientific Boxing

and

Self Defence

BY

TOMMY BURNS

(Champion of the World)

The Naval & Military Press Ltd

Published by

The Naval & Military Press Ltd
Unit 5 Riverside, Brambleside
Bellbrook Industrial Estate
Uckfield, East Sussex
TN22 1QQ England

Tel: +44 (0)1825 749494

www.naval-military-press.com
www.nmarchive.com

In reprinting in facsimile from the original, any imperfections are inevitably reproduced and the quality may fall short of modern type and cartographic standards.

DEDICATION.

I respectfully dedicate this book to the National Sporting Club, in memory of the hospitable and sportsmanlike manner in which that historic institution has treated me and the hosts of other American and Canadian boxers who have fought there.

Tommy Burns

CONTENTS.

Chap.		Page
	Preface	xiii.

I.—Why the New Style of Boxing is better than the Old   19

Boxing as a Profitable Calling—Why should Englishmen prefer to encourage Continental Wrestlers instead of fostering their Native Boxing Talent? — Mistakes of the English Style.

II.—Points which the Boxer should Cultivate ...   26

Footwork — Position — Feinting — How to Punch Effectively.

III.—Defence and Counter Hitting   36

Guarding and Blocking — My Favourite Guard—Slipping and Ducking—The Famous Shift—Counter Hitting.

IV.—Some Hints on Offensive and Defensive Tactics at Close Quarters   63

Hook Blows—The Upper Cut—The Hammer—The Kidney Punch—To Sum Up.

V.—Training on Scientific Lines, with Advice as to Diet   72

Short Walks are Best—The Way I Train—Sparring Practice—Ball Punching—Fight the Bag—Massage—The End of the Day—Final Hints for the Heavy-Weight.

CONTENTS.

Chap.		Page
VI.	On how to Train to Scale, together with Advice as to how to recognise and combat Overtraining or Staleness	96

When Training to Weight — Beware of Getting Stale.

| VII. | Ring Strategy and Tactics | 113 |

First Principles—Make your Opponent do all the Fighting—How to Meet a Rusher—Bill Squires' Charge—How to go into Action—Advantages of the Crouching Attitude—Hit Short Blows — In-Fighting Tactics — Don't Neglect the Body—Worrying Tactics—Change your Tactics—Making a Man Beat Himself—How to Fight a Round—The Quitter—When you get Knocked Down.

| VIII. | The Complete Second | 146 |

How a good Second may win a fight for his Principal—Spare your Principal all Avoidable Exertion.

| IX. | On Fouls | 158 |

| X. | The Boxer's Disease, which is too often the cause of his Downfall | 160 |

A Case in Point.

| XI. | Some Facts and Explanations | 163 |

The Correct Version of the incident at the National Sporting Club.

ILLUSTRATIONS.

	PAGE
Frontispiece : Tommy Burns	facing Title
A Characteristic Pose : Guard Out and Right ready for action	27
The American Crouch	31
Ducking, Left Lead and sending in Left to Body with Right to follow	39
Side Stepping : A Left Head Lead and hooking Left for Body	41
Left Body Counter to Left Head Lead	43
Right Side Step and Counter to Jaw in reply to Left Body Lead	45
Ducking a Right Head Lead and sending Right to Chin	47
Blocking Left for Body with Right Glove and sending Left Counter to Face	49
Blocking a Left Punch by pushing Opponent's Shoulder	51
Blocking Left Lead with Right Glove and Right follow with Shoulder push	53
A Right Cross Counter	59
Showing how a man can be "Outreached" ...	61
A Straight Left to Jaw, while a man is pulling his Left back for a Left Hook or Swing	67
A Right Body Jab (getting home in front of a Left Head Hook	69
Beating a Left Head Lead with a four inch Left Hook to Jaw	73

ILLUSTRATIONS.

	PAGE
Beating an Opponent's Left Body Hook with a Short Left Hook for Jaw	77
A Left Hook to Jaw at close range, Right ready for Upper Cut	81
Ball Punching—"A Left Jab"	85
do. do. Ready with the Right following a Left Jab	87
do. do. A Right Punch	89
do. do. A Straight Right	91
Stomach Exercise (I.)	97
do. do. (II.)	99
The Double Shift	105
Knocked Out by a Right "Cross"	107
A Left Head Lead "side stepped" so as to get into position for a Kidney Punch	109
Going into Action "covered up"	111
Taking Punch on Top of Head	117
Ducking a Left Swing and sending Right to Body	119
Fighting the Body in a "Clinch"	125
A Left Hook to the Stomach	127
Upper Cutting a Man who covers up	133
Feinting a Man to make him "fight"	135
Finishing a Man whom you have made "beat himself"	141
The Right Way to Take the Count	143
The Great Burns—Squires Fight	149
A. F. Bettinson, Esq.	153
Eugene Corri, Esq.	167
"Gunner" Moir	169

PREFACE

I have set out to write this book, as it has been pointed out to me that, by so doing, I can best answer those gentlemen who, for reasons best known to themselves, have, on the one hand, sought to belittle my achievements, and who, on the other hand, have done their best to use me as a tool whereby they might stir up ill-feeling between England and America.

A certain incident at the National Sporting Club on the occasion of my fight with Moir gave rise to a lot of discussion, and, owing to a misapprehension of the facts of the case, caused some comments among the spectators. As soon as the members of the Club were informed of the truth of the matter, they at once, in the most sportsman-like manner, testified their regret that any notice whatever should have been taken of it, and I, therefore, concluded that the whole thing was over and done with.

But some gentleman concluded that he had come across a mine of " good copy," and hastened to seize the opportunity to blast forth a whole series of inventions, which he cabled over to the American Press, which promptly issued a wildly absurd narrative of the events in question.

This farrago of nonsense was neither complimentary nor agreeable to myself, but I don't mind that. What I *do* mind, however, is the wicked libel on one of the finest body of sportsmen in the whole world.

They have been " white," clear " white " to me, from the first moment I met them, and I would like them and all the world to know how I appreciate their kindness and sporting behaviour. I have dedicated this book to them as a public acknowledgment of my feelings, and I can only regret that I have no means of making a handsomer one.

My explanation of the incident above alluded to I have felt myself compelled to publish on account of the fact that certain English papers, whose representatives were actual eye-witnesses of the scene in question, have yet allowed themselves, apparently, to gather their ideas from the accounts published in the American Press, which were written by a man who was not even in the Club at the time.

Why these London editors should fancy that an American reporter could see better through the walls of the building, or from the bar of a neighbouring hostelry, than they could themselves from the distance of a few feet, I am unable to divine, but they have, nevertheless, quite recently issued a fresh version of the scene, which does not tally with their first account so much as it does with the American version.

Now, as people rarely read prefaces, and as I wish everybody to learn the truth about this matter, I am giving my account later on, where no reader can help seeing it, but those who do read prefaces will be able to discover why I shall subsequently lay so much stress on the matter.

One other reason has actuated me in writing this book, and that is because I don't want people to think I am making the bald-headed eagle scream when I claim supremacy for the American boxer, or for the American athlete generally. I do claim this supremacy, but there are reasons for it. It is not a superiority of men so much, as a superiority of method and of circumstances, or, perhaps, at bottom, of circumstances only. For, in the States, we take all things more seriously than you Britishers do.

If a boxer or any other brand of athlete wishes to demonstrate his skill, he can find any number of opportunities to do so. Take myself, for instance. I am not 27 years old yet, and yet I have fought over 50 battles since the year 1900, an average of, say, 8 or more a year. What English heavy-weight gets anything like these opportunities for practice?

Take Gunner Moir, for instance. Why, including his fight with me, he has only fought 4 men in two years. That isn't his fault, but his misfortune, for it's practice alone that makes perfect.

All the rest of a British champion's time, and his only chance of making a living outside actual fighting, is exhibition sparring, *i.e.*, putting on the gloves with a man who isn't in the same class with him, and who he must take care not to hurt. About the worse practice he could have, for it makes him fight *down* to the level of his exhibition partners (so as to make anything like a good equal show for the spectators), and it isn't possible for him to help deteriorating instead of improving as he should be doing.

He gets to look at the Exhibition business as the chief thing to be considered, and when he grows old and becomes a trainer or instructor, preaches that style as being the one his pupils should adopt. There's a reason for British inferiority, particularly in the heavy-weight class, in which you have fewer annual battles than in any other. I don't think that you need trouble to find another.

I have called this book "Scientific Boxing and Self-defence," and I want that first word to sink into your minds. Just get rid of the idea that Boxing is brutal. It isn't. It's a business in which brains count more than anything, and, properly worked, it isn't such a bad business to take up. There's money to be made at it, and if you are real good you can make it quicker than you can at most other professions. Which is fortunate, because you have to retire at a comparatively early age. But, if you have been just ordinarily careful and have remembered that in a few years' time you won't be earning as much as you are now, you can save up enough to start you in another business if you want to, or can rest quiet and content as a gentleman of means, if that fancy tickles you.

I went into the boxing business more or less by accident, and have stuck to it, because I found that I could make more money that way than I could in any other. Show me the same amount of dollars as quickly earned in another calling, in which I could shine, and I am done with the ring, but, until I see that, I shall cling on to this profession, until Time or some other more formidable antagonist puts me out of it.

Jem Roche, perhaps, you will say. Well, he may, or even Jack Johnson. But, whoever it is, I can promise him that he'll have to go all the way. I didn't win the World's Championship easily, and I don't mean to give it up if I can help it. Sure, I won't give it up tamely.

CHAPTER I.

Why the New Style of Boxing is better than the Old.

That England has held the World's Boxing Championship is, of course, a well-known fact.

That she will hold it again is by no means an impossibility or an improbability.

But the fact nevertheless remains that since Jem Mace's time the championship title has been held on the other side of the Atlantic, and that, despite various attempts on the part of several English representatives, the nearest approach which Englishmen have ever made towards regaining the honour has been its capture by the British born, naturalised American citizen—Bob Fitzsimmons.

I can well understand that Britons should be asking themselves why this should be.

The United Kingdom can still breed men as strong and plucky as any she ever bred, but the trouble is that she would appear to have lost the capacity for turning out scientific heavy-weight boxers.

Various critics have offered different explanations of this state of affairs, but the simplest of all, and one which seems to me to have been quite overlooked, would seem to have originated in the wave of sentimentality which passed over Great Britain about the middle of the nineteenth century, and the influences of which have by no means yet evaporated, and which has kept men of higher grades of intelligence from entering the lists.

Boxing as a Profitable Calling.

The man of good education, accustomed to think for himself, and possessed of a fair capacity for initiative, in fact, the very man qualified to shine in the Boxing arena, hesitates to don the small gloves and contents himself with joining an Amateur Boxing Club. The only contests for which he enters are such competitions as his club may promote, and which are almost invariably contested in a genuine sporting spirit and on strictly conventional lines. The style, the science, the very blows and guards are all conventional, originality being neither desired nor encouraged.

You will, of course, turn round here and say that this is exactly what you want, and that you have no desire to see the professional taking the centre of the picture.

The amateur side of the question is the one that mainly appeals to you, because among amateurs alone can boxing be contested in a purely sporting spirit.

Well, I am not so sure of that altogether. I have seen contests between professionals which were distinguished throughout by the fairest and most sportsmanlike spirit, and I have also seen amateur contests which could not be so described. But that is by the way. The point to which I wish chiefly to draw attention is that if you persistently regard your professional element in any sport as something in the nature of a necessary evil, then must you rest satisfied to see the International Championships in those sports departing from your shores. How many sports are there in which the Genuine Amateur can hope to hold his own with the Professional, or with the Amateur who is such only in name?

You cannot enjoy the fun pure and simple and the glory at the same time. You must admit that unless you devote your most serious attention to all your athletic pursuits, you must be prepared to admit the supremacy of some other country in those sports, of which the amusing side only appeals to you.

There is, surely, nothing disgraceful in being a Professional Boxer. Any one of your prominent amateurs, who finds himself able to hold his own fairly well with the Club Professional, and who has no very profitable business pursuit at his fingers' ends, might do far worse than match himself for a few trial bouts with local professionals.

He will have to sacrifice his amateur status, of course, but then, unless he is a confirmed "pot-hunter," that should not be such a serious sacrifice ; while, supposing him to be successful in these trial encounters, he will have gone a fair journey on the road to making a decent living at the business for which he is best suited.

He will have acquired confidence, for one thing ; no mean asset that. Then he will have gained experience by which he should benefit, especially in the development of his Ring Craft. A few more similar encounters and he will then have good grounds on which to decide whether he shall go into such serious training as will qualify him to emerge successfully from any important match which may be proposed to him, but which will also entail his throwing up his existing means of livelihood for the Boxing Profession pure and simple, at which, however, if successful, he will earn considerably more money than he would probably do as a clerk, shop assistant, or mechanic.

But, if he is to establish fame and to make money in England, there must be better encouragement for him. Your English light, feather and bantam-weights can certainly find a fair number of opponents, but your heavy-weights——

The British heavy-weight, if he would acquire any

high degree of science, must almost of necessity migrate to America, in search of those finer points of the game which can only be gained from actual practice with cleverer men than himself.

So many Englishmen still look on the art of Self-Defence as being a brutal one, that the British heavy-weight champion is denied opportunities to prove his worth.

The National Sporting Club has done what it could in this direction, but one swallow cannot make a summer, nor one club alone provide a sufficient series of big heavy-weight battles such as is needed for the development of British heavy-weight talent.

I notice that it has been suggested that an Association should be formed which would govern Professional Boxing in England, licensing clubs and registering boxers.

If this proposal is taken up and carried through, I venture to prophesy that it would prove the best incentive to Boxing which the Science has ever been accorded in England.

With a President, such as the one suggested, viz., Lord Lonsdale, and duly supported by such genuine sportsmen as the members of the National Sporting Club, the proposed Association would provide a most satisfactory guarantee that all contests brought off under its supervision were perfectly fair and above-board. That there was no suspicion of "fake" or arrangement about them, such as too often attaches to wrestling matches, for instance.

Why should Englishmen prefer to encourage Continental Wrestlers instead of Fostering their Native Boxing Talent ?

Just reckon up how many *Great* Wrestling Matches you have paid to witness, which have been either foregone conclusions, before the men faced each other on the mat, or, concerning which, some scandalous *arrangement* has not subsequently been disclosed.

Now, these *Great* Wrestling Matches are almost invariably contested by big, fleshy Germans, Russians, Turks, or Frenchmen, whose claims to championship (?) honours would hardly stand investigation, and yet you roll up by the thousand to enthuse over them.

In what way can Wrestling be said to be so superior to Boxing, that you will enable a foreign " knight of the mat " to make a large or a small fortune out of what are, only too frequently, purely exhibition bouts, and will leave your native-born boxers to earn a precarious existence by boxing in booths at fairs, or in penny gaffs?

Surely a genuine Boxing contest is more interesting to look at than a faked Wrestling Display! and as for brutality (which I have heard mentioned as a reason for boxing matches not being so profitable as Wrestling Matches) well, I will wager that there is more brutality, savagery, and dirty, tricky business indulged in by the highest class Professional Wrestlers, than you will ever see even in a fourth-rate Boxing Contest.

Whatever the Art of Self-Defence may have been in the old Prize Ring days, I am open to maintain that it is far from being brutal to-day.

It has not stayed still, any more than anything else. Fistic battles nowadays are not to be gained by sheer brute strength and indifference to physical pain.

The Champion Boxer must study how to avoid receiving punishment even more carefully than he must devote his attention to its infliction.

He can even, as I hope to prove later on, win a contest without having meted out anything very severe to his opponent, provided he be clever enough and, above all, in perfect condition.

But, in order to acquire this necessary science, he must be unremitting in his practice, and must neglect no opportunity of practising with men of every variety of style.

Mistakes of the English Style.

From what I have seen over here in England, where your Boxing instructors make their greatest mistake, is in insisting on a certain stereotyped style.

In your schools or gymnasia you will notice that every pupil seems to not only invariably take up the same position against any and every opponent, but to lead, guard, counter, side-step, duck, etc., all on the same rule and pattern.

One man may be slightly quicker than another, is *better trained*, hits harder, or times and directs his blows better, and by these means establishes his superiority.

But let him run up against an antagonist who adopts different methods, comes at him in the American crouching or other style, which his own mentor would have termed highly unorthodox, and he will be uncertain what to do.

His confusion grows if his man shows a total disregard for the good old principle of leading off with the left, or if he keeps up a perpetual feinting with both hands, swaying and slipping from side to side in a motion which may be indicative of either attack or retreat, until, after a varied exhibition of what the old style pugilist would describe as " shocking form," the traditionally trained man becomes so frightfully bewildered as to be practically defeated almost without having been hit at all.

Things are ordered differently in America, as they also

are by several English feather and bantam-weights, such as Owen Moran, Jim Driscoll, Joe Bowker, etc.

In the States, for instance, there are numerous well attended schools and gymnasia in every city of importance, where the instructor, beyond handing out the rudiments and simple rules, will rather encourage his pupils to teach each other, confining his instructions mainly to pointing out mistakes which they have made in their several bouts and how these may best be remedied.

In all branches of industry, improvements and new devices are most frequently discovered by accident, and a smart professor may often notice that the rawest novice has evolved instinctively an original method of conducting or countering an attack, which, carefully developed and polished, may establish a new school of boxing altogether.

The great John L. Sullivan has been credited with the discovery of the "knock-out" blow on the point of the jaw, and certainly, from the time he first put it into practice, the present era of boxing may be said to date.

Fitzsimmons, on the other hand, established the superiority of body-fighting to head-fighting, and as Jeffries followed the lead thus set him, all boxers are now practising and developing this branch of the business.

As I have already mentioned more than once, Boxing or Glove-fighting has passed out of its early stages of brute force, and indomitable endurance into the era of brain work and science.

Brains are of more importance than fists to-day.

CHAPTER II.

Points which the Boxer should cultivate.

Footwork.

The first essential of a Scientific Boxer must be quick and clever footwork.

I would, I think, get a pupil quick on his feet almost before I started teaching him how to hit or guard, for, unless he can get a move on him as quick as lightning and can keep on moving all the time if need be, he will need some most extraordinary other advantages to become a champion.

In modern Boxing, speed is nearly everything, and I have always considered my success to be primarily due to the fact that Lacrosse and Hockey had taught me to be spry and smart on my feet before I ever thought of donning a pair of boxing gloves.

So I would advise the young ambitious **Boxer** to cultivate a taste for such games as will develop rapid footwork. From my own experience, I should imagine that Lacrosse and Hockey are about best for this department, but I should not be surprised to learn that Football or even Lawn Tennis, if played at tip-top speed throughout, would serve almost as well.

A Characteristic Pose: Guard out and Right ready for action.

In any event, they will accustom the novice to be always " on his toes," and get him into the habit of being so whenever he is sparring. The great thing, however, is to get him into the trick of it, and the rest will follow naturally.

Position.

Then, as the novice goes into action, he should be careful to balance his weight equally, so as to be ready to move quickly any way. The chin should be kept fairly low down, ready to cuddle in to the chest if need be, for the chin is the most vulnerable point.

The veriest novice may " put out " a champion with a wild swing, if he only lands " right " and lands hard enough. As a rule, the left arm and shoulder are held out in advance, with the elbow bent and the fist on a level with or slightly higher than the elbow; the right arm held across the body, covering " the mark " or diaphragm, the right hand just below the left breast. The left foot is advanced pointing towards one's opponent, with the right foot at right angles to it, and from 18 inches to 2 feet in the rear. Legs slightly bent, and left arm kept moving easily backward and forward.

That is the academic position, and possesses the advantages of presenting but a small target, and also of gaining such others as may be presented by one's full limit of height and reach.

But as already stated, I have but little faith in stereotyped forms. I would advise anyone studying Scientific Boxing to try and accustom himself to all manner of positions, provided that they do not hamper his freedom of movement.

The more versatile a boxer is and the greater variety of poses which he can adopt with ease, the greater chance he has of puzzling and confusing, and, consequently, of defeating his opponent.

The accompanying illustrations will show a favourite position of my own and also the celebrated American "crouch," which has the advantage of forcing an adversary to hit "down" at you, and thus enable you to take his blows on the top of your head (where they won't hurt you much), while you will be in a favourable position to get well in to him, between his arms if possible, with all his body open to your attack.

Feinting.

Then, again, the old-time instructor attaches the first importance to correct "leading," *i.e.*, initial attacks directed at your opponent's head or body, whether these be with the left, right, or both hands. This would appear to be justified by the fact that in amateur competitions lasting three rounds, where the combatants are fairly equal, the decision is awarded to the man who has done most leading.

In spite of this, it must be evident that little advantage is to be gained by a series of "leads," all of which are either guarded, slipped, or countered.

Before the boxer can "lead" or hit in any way to advantage, he must, by some feint or manœuvre, "draw" his opponent—that is to say, lure him into such a position as will yield an opening for a telling blow.

Hence, to my mind, the primary importance of skilful "feinting." This can be done in a variety of ways. With the hands, with the feet, with the eyes even, and by a mere change of attitude.

The American Crouch.

Keep moving, especially from the moment you face your man. If you are quick on your feet and a fairly good judge of " distance " you can feint to go " in " to him, so as to lure him into a lead himself, which you can slip, side-step, duck, or get back out of the way of, with the probability that he will slightly lose his balance and enable you to get home with an effective punch.

The boxer should try and train himself into a perpetual series of feints, keeping it going all the time. He can, in time, so perfect himself in this department as to be able to keep it up with very little comparative exertion to himself, while he is tricking his opponent into doing all the fighting, inducing him to waste punch after punch on the air, thereby tiring and wearying himself, to say nothing of so confusing and bewildering him as to make him leave any number of openings.

How to Punch Effectively.

The quickest punches are necessarily the straight arm ones. They will always get there quicker than any round arm swing, and the best, hardest, and most effective are those which travel over the shortest distance.

A big " swing " or a long, straight drive right out from the shoulder may look very taking and attractive, but believe me your opponent will vastly prefer receiving that kind of blow to one of those short half-arm jabs, which only travel about a foot or at most 18 inches, and which have the full weight of the shoulder behind them.

Certain critics have been very severe on my style, which some have described as " fair middle-class boxing." They have denied me any particular credit for the majority of my victories (although they were generally ready to prophesy that my antagonist would simply " eat me "), and then have run down those very antagonists for going down and out so easily.

They may possibly be right in their contentions, and the whole Science of Boxing may be degenerate as they style it, and not better and more advanced than it ever was, as I believe it to be; but, nevertheless, I would like to remind them that, in their haste to decry me, they have quite forgotten to account for the "ease" with which they have noted that I have achieved my successes.

Marvin Hart, Jack O'Brien, Bill Squires, "Gunner" Moir, and Jack Palmer were all boomed to the skies before I beat them. They had all established pretty decent reputations as boxers or as fighters, and were acclaimed as such.

If they were the "lemons" which they have since been described as being, what must the men have been like at whose cost they gained their fame?

No, they went down and out or quit the game, because they had cause.

I have no desire to blow my own trumpet, but only to remind my critics and incidentally to assure my readers that it is not the blow which comes home with a flourish and a swish that makes the other man wish he wasn't there.

It is the quick, short jab on the proper spot which is felt, even though it isn't often seen.

If you have to lead over a distance, send in your left or right as the case may be, either as a feint or on genuine business bent, spring in after it, and send in a quick, short jab either with the same or the other hand immediately afterwards.

Practice this double leading all you can, and bring it into action especially when you have feinted your man into an open or slightly puffed condition. Again, if you have led-off and your man is following you up after it, you can often bring him up sharp with this species of postman's knock, which will gain in force by his coming in to meet it. You may even, with advantage, feint springing back, so as to trick him into the follow up, and then stay where you are and hit him again.

In all cases you should spring in close when sending in a double lead, as, supposing you were to fail with your intentions, your only escape from punishment will be in a " clinch." Hitting out twice in this fashion is sometimes even more effective when both hands are brought into play, but when this is done the first hand should automatically " cover up " as the second goes in.

CHAPTER III.

Defence and Counter Hitting.

"Guarding" and "Blocking."

When stopping a blow, which you can neither slip nor duck, do your utmost to contrive that this shall be taken on the glove itself. There is absolutely no reason why you should try and get your arm bruised in stopping a punch; for, if you have accurately guessed your opponent's intentions, you should be able to get your open glove—palm outwards—well over the point aimed at by the time his fist arrives. If, however, he is leading at your head, raise your guarding arm until your wrist is level or slightly higher than your forehead, keeping the arm fairly straight. This will glance his arm off and often enable you to get inside, but I would in nearly all cases recommend you to slip or duck the blow in preference to any style of parrying it.

My Favourite Guard.

My favourite method of warding off a blow, however, is one which I never remember to have seen described in any Boxing Text Book, and to have rarely seen practised by other boxers, despite the fact that I have always found it wonderfully simple and effective.

But it must be executed with the utmost rapidity, or disaster will result. My guard may almost be described as a counter, with the advantage that it hasn't so far to travel, doesn't lay you open to a re-counter, and is, if quickly brought into play and repeatedly employed, almost as effective as the ordinary counter, and, if I may say so, infinitely prettier.

Be sure of your opponent's intentions, and then, just as his arm comes forward at you, jump lightly and slightly forward, and push at his hitting shoulder or upper arm.

If his blow is by way of being a round-arm blow or swing, you ought to be able to get your push in easily and in good time. Greater accuracy in timing and direction is, of course, needed against a straight drive, but the effect is the same.

You will break the force of his blow before it has gathered speed, and so prevent its arrival, while you will, at the same time, not only avoid all the jar of its impact on either your arm, head, or body, but will throw your adversary more or less off his balance, and thus lay him open to reprisals.

Besides this, by repeatedly making use of this method of baulking him, you will tire and irritate him as well, in a manner which you will find highly satisfactory to yourself.

By the way, I have advised you to jump in a little when using this push, but you will, of course, be guided here largely by circumstances. So much will depend on your relative positions at the time, that is to say, whether you are placed favourably for him to hit you, or for you to push his arm or shoulder. In such cases you will, of course, either stand firm or even jump slightly back, in which cases your push will naturally lose considerably in force.

In any event, I look upon this method of stopping a blow as one of the most valuable moves in my *repertoire*, and I would strongly recommend all my readers to practise it as much as possible.

Get your sparring partner to try all manner of punches at you—left and right hand leads and counters, round arm swings, etc.—and accustom yourself to timing and stopping them in this manner. At first, perhaps, you will get knocked about a bit before you get the hang of it, but once you have mastered the trick, you will, I am sure, find that you have not paid any too dear a price for the value received.

Slipping and Ducking.

This department of modern Boxing is another into which rapidity of foot-work and quickness of movement generally is of the utmost importance.

The boxer must keep well on his toes if he wants to be smart at side-stepping, and if he means to be a champion he must be highly proficient, for he will find his time so taken up in warding off body punches, that he will be glad to rely chiefly on the duck or slip in order to save his head.

For instance, when a man leads at your head, and you are well within range of his fist, it is wisest to shift your frontispiece to the right and to, at the same time, step about 18 inches to the right. This will generally place you well for a left drive at his body or head, which should be delivered the while you turn or pivot round on the ball of the right foot, swinging your left round to add force to your blow.

It is not advisable, however, to get into the habit of always side-stepping either right or left. Practice variety in this as in all other moves. Remember, that if your man gets to know that you will always act in the same way to a certain move of his, then he will (if worth his salt) lay traps for you in that direction.

Ducking Left Head Lead, and sending in Left to Body with Right to follow.

Side Stepping: A Left Head Lead and Hooking Left for Body.

Left Body Counter to Left Head Lead.

Right Side Step and Counter to Jaw, in reply to Left Body Lead.

Ducking a Right Head Lead and sending Right to Chin.

Blocking Left for Body with Right Glove and sending Left Counter to Face.

Blocking a Left Punch by pushing Opponent's Shoulder.

Blocking Left Lead with Right Glove and Right follow with Shoulder Push.

The object which you must keep chiefly in view is the discovery of his weaknesses—not the exposure of your own.

Therefore, vary all your replies to all his moves. Slip sometimes to the right and at others to the left. Stand and duck only at others. Guard at times; but when you do slip, always bear in mind the opportunities presented for a good pivot blow, and remember, also, that if this should fail to come off, that you are almost always well placed to get in the "shift."

The Famous "Shift."

This celebrated punch, which from the frequency with which Bob Fitzsimmons employed it was formerly called the "Fitzsimmons' Shift," is delivered either with the right off the left foot, or with the left off the right foot, bringing the other leg and shoulder rapidly up behind the fist. It is, of course, a half-arm straight jab, depending for its force on the swing of the body behind it, and not on the force of any hit as such. Once the blow has landed on the body the fist can be slid upwards to the chin or jaw.

The Double Shift, an illustration of which is shown, is merely an elaboration of the shift itself. The boxer has side-stepped a lead and swung round to deliver a pivot, but his opponent has been too quick for him. As shown in the illustration, he will now drive in his left, bringing his right leg up behind to add force to the blow and with it the right arm, which should be aided by a forward left swing.

Counter Hitting.

This method of getting home on your opponent is generally far more severe than any amount of "leading" or initial attack hitting, since its effect is enhanced, I may say doubled, by the impact of the oncoming body. The recipient of a good " counter " blow comes forward to meet the punch, instead of going slightly away from it, as he would be if he were merely desirous of avoiding punishment.

The whole secret of successful counter hitting consists in accurate timing and anticipation of an opponent's intentions.

The methods in which a counter can be brought into operation are even more numerous than the variety of "leads," and most of these methods can be employed, if desired, in reply to almost any lead.

Suppose your opponent to have led at your head with his left.

You can either duck to the right and slightly forward, sending your own left straight to his head, or you can parry with your right and similarly send in the left. This has its advantages, as much body swing is apt to be lost over the duck, but against that may be set off the defenceless position of your body, supposing his lead to have been only a feint. The left head counter, by the way, is the least forceful of all, and is not, as a rule, particularly effective, unless it comes full in the nose or mouth, The right foot should remain stationary in delivering this blow.

Should the left lead be a round arm swing, a right counter to the exposed chin will be found very effective, and, in many cases, will result in a " knock-out " ; but, if you are standing at the moment with your left foot forward, you will often find yourself late in landing.

The left head counter comes in very useful as a reply to a left body " lead," if you are standing in the crouching attitude or have your body well drawn back, for, in that case, there is no necessity to guard, as owing to

SCIENTIFIC BOXING AND SELF-DEFENCE. 57

your opponent's head coming forward, the counter, if accurately timed, should land far sooner than the lead itself.

Body counters, either right or left, are tremendously effective replies, especially to blows directed at the head, which must in such cases be successfully dodged. The mere process of ducking either right or left will add force to the swing with which the opposite fist is brought into play.

Then, again, many boxers have a trick of throwing up their guarding arm to protect their faces when leading, and this habit of theirs leaves the body well open to attack.

The cross-counters, right and left, are two of the most severe blows which a boxer can deliver, the first especially so. It is safe to say that the majority of " knock-outs " have been secured with this punch. The point aimed at is the left angle of the jaw on the point of the chin, and the blow comes in across your opponent's arm over his left shoulder. In reply to a left head lead, it is practically unstoppable, and can only be robbed of its effect by sinking the chin well behind the buttress of the shoulder when leading, that is, supposing your lead itself to have failed in stopping the counter, by arriving first. The man delivering the counter must duck his head forward to the left. He has, of course, to chance getting this out of the way in time. Care should also be exercised to make the counter travel over as short a space as possible, and to get plenty of shoulder behind your fist.

English boxers, as a rule, " swing " this blow rather, and so lose good and valuable time, besides wasting a good deal of its force. Then, again, they pull their left elbow and shoulder back presumably to gain force for a big drive, to aid their right punch. To a certain extent this may add some force to the cross-counter itself, but it has the demerit of leaving the face open to an upper cut, and the body to a right jab, supposing the left lead to have been a feint to gain an opening for either of the right arm blows.

This, by the way, is not a bad feint, provided it be executed properly. The apparent left lead will tempt the other man into trying the right cross, and can be converted into a shoulder push, such as I described in my remarks on guarding, while the right is used with telling effect, either as a body punch or in an upper cut, well into the face which has come down to meet it.

For these reasons, if for no others, the right cross should be made as short and quick as possible, and the left arm should be held covering up, in case of accidents, for, provided a man knows how, he can jab quite as effectively, if not more so, from the short range as he can with the long drive, obtained by pulling back the shoulder and elbow.

In all cases, when leading (either as a feint or otherwise) in such fashion as to invite a right cross, drop your chin well beneath the protection of your shoulder, and remember that your right is there to stop uppercuts or body jabs. It may not seem easy to combine the lead and head duck, but it is far better to take the right cross on the back of your head than on your jaw, and, in the majority of cases, you can depend pretty safely on the blow being attempted, if you even apparently lay yourself open to it, since it is the one blow of all which is most likely to terminate a battle; and no boxer is fond enough of the risks which will crop up every minute to neglect a chance of bringing a contest to a summary conclusion.

The left cross is, properly speaking, a hook hit, that is to say, it is a blow delivered with a crooked elbow about the level of the shoulder.

A Right Cross-Counter.

Showing how a Man can be "Outreached" merely by Turning Sideways.

CHAPTER IV.

Some Hints on Offensive and Defensive Tactics at close quarters.

Hook Blows.

These are a sort of cross between the swinging and the straight blows, and are far more effective than the former. Firstly, because they get home quicker; secondly, because they are bent arm blows; and, thirdly and chiefly, because they are jabs, which, as I have already mentioned, are far more painful things to receive than any swing, although they may not have that appearance.

Another advantage of the hook is that it is often liable to be mistaken for a swing, in which case the other man will in all probability duck forward a bit late, and so run right into your fist. On the other hand, should he try to parry it by raising his arm to guard the supposed swing, you will come in under his arm with almost equal effect.

The blow starts as though a swing were intended, but stops short almost at once, and slips in for the face in a slightly upward direction. It is by no means an easy blow to guard, save by a straight, well-timed counter, and it has played a big part in the annals of the Ring.

The great John L. Sullivan went down before its frequent use when he was knocked out by Corbett. It can be sent in either right or left, at fairly close quarters, particularly when your opponent has an arm drawn back low down, or raised to guard the swing. It should be worked as far as possible from inside the other man's guard, though it can come as, already mentioned, in the form of a cross, when it passes over instead of under the arm, and may then, perhaps, be knocked up, or the wrist or hand damaged on the top or back of the skull.

The Upper Cut.

This most effective blow is another species of counter sent in its most effective form, in reply to a head lead, with the head lowered. Cover your own face, get in quick, and hit upwards from a bent elbow position with the other hand. In this case the force is chiefly derived from the abdominal muscles, which makes it rather an exhausting blow to bring often into play. It is useful, nevertheless, against a man who will persist in "covering up," and is often the only way to get at him; but even then, unless careful, you are liable to bring your wrist into painful contact with his elbow.

By the way, if you can count confidently on your opponent trying to upper-cut you, whenever an opportunity presents itself, it isn't a bad plan to try and tempt him to try one on. Feint as though you are going to lead with your head down in nice position for a right upper-cut, and then suddenly throw the head back and drive at his face with your left.

Another method of tricking a man who is fond of using his right in this particular fashion is to drop your head forward and make a feint of going for his face with your left, then stop the lead and cover with left glove, while sending in the right to his left ribs or to the mark, if possible.

The left hand can also be sent in to the body after a feint at the face with head down, which has drawn your opponent into a left hand " cut," but in this case you should step well to the right so as to get at the unprotected left side.

The Hammer.

This is a useful blow sometimes in close fighting. The right hand is the one generally used, as it is the one most frequently best placed for it, but either arm, if covering up the body aslant, can be smashed downwards in hammer fashion at the point of your opponent's chin. If you have your arms inside your opponent's and have not quite got into a clinch, you have just the time and opportunity to bring it into most effective operation.

The Kidney Punch.

This blow, which certain persons here in England would seem to want to have declared a foul blow, is one of the most effective open to a boxer. I know no reason why it should be forbidden, especially as it is often about the only blow which can be brought into play against a man who persistently clinches and is fond of going to sleep with his chin on your chest or shoulder. He is able to protect both his body and face in this position, and can, moreover, cover up his ribs with his elbows.

Supposing him to have hooked on to your shoulders, and upper arms as well, you are practically unable to do anything, save wait for the referee to separate you, often only to find him hugging you again.

There is only one method of dealing with these demonstrations of affection, and that is to see that you keep one arm free as he comes in, so that you can tap him pretty severely over the kidneys every time.

A few visitations in that region will make him far less loving, and will either make him anxious to quit altogether, or persuade him to stand up and fight.

You can also get this blow in fairly forcefully by slipping a lead well to the right or left, as the case may be, coming forward as well as sideways so that his arm shoots past, then push his striking arm a trifle, so as to turn his back more towards you, when you can let go good and hard with the other hand at the tender spot.

If your punch comes off quick and good and in the right place, you won't have much more trouble. He may go right out then and there, but even if he doesn't do so, he won't be in any good condition to stall off any subsequent attack you may wish to put into operation.

To Sum Up.

I have now, I believe, run through all the principal blows, guards, feints, etc., which a boxer should study up and get acquainted with for use in any and every emergency, but before passing on to the items of training and the strategic and tactical side of Scientific Boxing, I would like to advise all my readers to get well posted in the art of clinching.

I have tried to advise you on the steps you should take against a man who persistently clinches himself, but, on the other hand, it must not be forgotten that this is often the only method by which a boxer can escape severe punishment.

In the old Prize Ring days, a clinch invariably led up to a wrestle, and, consequently, unless the prize-fighter was pretty useful at the grappling game, there was no advantage in his seeking safety by this method.

The influence of this may possibly account for the general failure of British boxers to take the same advantage of a clinch that Americans do.

A Straight Left to Jaw, while a Man is pulling his Left back for a Left Hook or Swing (showing the superior speed of a straight blow).

A Right Body Jab getting home in front of a Left Head Hook.

For instance, I have noticed that your men, when getting to close quarters and not well suited either to get clear away, or to put in a good punch, frequently drop their hands too soon, and, consequently, get handed out a nasty jab, which they might easily have avoided by getting wisely into holds.

Take it as a maxim that, whether you have got home or no, either with lead or counter, your hands must never be dropped until you have got clear away. If you can't do this easily, or don't think that you can do it safely, get close in to your man, with your face on his chest—if shorter than he—or on his shoulder otherwise, and clip his arms and waist as well as you can. It may not look over pretty, but unless you overdo it, and so invite disqualification, it is surely foolish to run the risk of bad punishment and a possible defeat, just for the sake of displaying your airs and graces.

A scientific boxing bout is not a brutal exhibition; but, then, it isn't a parlour game either!

CHAPTER V.

Training on Scientific Lines, with Advice as to Diet.

Tradition dies hard, since man is a creature of habit, and for many reasons it is no matter for surprise that traditional methods should still be popular in England, despite the plentiful evidence which goes to prove that they are out-of-date.

After all, you Britishers invented the Noble Art of Self-defence, and were cocks of the walk in that particular branch of Athletics for considerably over a century.

Yours is a country in which life marches along well-established grooves, and you are, therefore, naturally reluctant to confess that there are better methods than those which have become almost hallowed by custom.

All your Boxers practically are British born, of British stock, and have been trained on British lines by men who were themselves trained in much the same fashion, and who consequently preach the same doctrines as were preached to them in their youth.

Consequently, your boxers go through much the same preparation as your Wrestlers, not impossibly, perhaps; because, not so very long ago, your boxers had to be pretty good wrestlers in order to distinguish themselves in the Prize Ring.

On the other side of the Atlantic, however, it has long been recognised that a good Wrestler can never make a good Boxer. The meat of the one is poison to the other.

Wrestling calls for big, bunching muscles, heavy

Beating a Left Head Lead with a 4-inch Left Hook to Jaw (showing the advantage of the short blow).

shoulders, strong lifting powers, etc., all of which are handicaps to a boxer.

The one requires strength above all things outside skill, and the other speed above all things, since speed at boxing is practically identical with skill.

To that end, the boxer needs to have his muscles as supple and loose as possible, and should carefully avoid all such methods as training with weights, heavy dumbbells, rope climbing, parallel bars and other apparatus such as will thicken and develop his chest and shoulders certainly, but at the cost of giving him a tendency to become muscle bound.

Short Walks are Best.

It is recorded that the first English Boxer who ever underwent a special preparation for an important contest was Tom Cribb, who was taken in hand by the celebrated Capt. Barclay, the principal feature of whose system was a daily 30 mile walk, followed by two good mile spins. The process was completed by a walk from his training quarters to the scene of action, the total distance covered on this tramp being some 300 miles in about a fortnight.

No man had ever previously entered the Prize Ring in such grand condition as Cribb did on that occasion, with the result that long daily walks have since that day seemingly become accepted as being an indispensable item in a British Boxer's preparation.

Now, a long 20 or 30 mile daily walk may develop a man's strength and stamina, and will certainly improve his wind. But, on the other hand, such a procedure cannot fail to make him slow and plodding.

No man can start off for a tramp of that length at tip-top speed ; nor, if he does so, can he hope to keep up. Besides which, the weariness inseparable from such a lengthy, monotonous exertion cannot fail to take all the zest out of him for his gymnasium work, which is the more important part of his preparation.

I have devoted so much space to this walking proposition, because it seems to me to be about the most serious mistake which English Boxers make in their training, and because I have wished to bring that fact home to them as clearly as I possibly can.

The Way I Train.

The methods which I have followed ever since I found myself unable to get down to middle-weight with anything like comfort, have been simple but effective.

Before starting proceedings, I take a fairly strong dose of salts in order to thin out my blood and expel all impurities out of my system, and generally to get myself into good fettle for the process of training itself.

I get out somewhere into the country, into hilly districts, such as Hampstead Heath for choice (if I were resident in London), and then carry out the following routine.

I am up about 8 in the morning, and breakfast generally on oranges, a couple of eggs, toast and tea, though I may vary this with a dish of stewed prunes or rhubarb, in both of which, and the latter especially, I am a firm believer.

Then comes my roadwork. This never exceeds 7 or 8 miles at the outside (but rarely more than 5), and consists of a brisk mile walk as fast as I can go, then sprint for a hundred yards or so, at racing speed, then a fast walk again, and so on. It is advisable to cover as much hilly ground as you can, both to develop your leg muscles and to deepen your chest and your wind. Back at my quarters again, I am rubbed down, have a light cold

Beating an Opponent's Left Body Hook with a short Left Hook for Jaw (showing the advantage of a short blow).

shower bath, and am massaged thoroughly, of which more anon.

Then dinner or lunch, whichever you like to call it. This consists of roast beef or lamb, or a chop or steak, with peas, tomatoes, toast and tea. No potatoes or bread.

After a rest comes the gymnasium at 3 o'clock, and the more serious work of the day.

This comprises any amount of shadow fighting, to develop my speed and keep me brisk and spry on my toes.

Then comes skipping and exercises for the stomach muscles, to strengthen and develop these so as to qualify them to resist the thumping they may not impossibly receive in the actual contest. These movements consist of lying on my back on the floor, raising my legs to right angles with my body, then sitting up, by muscular exertion alone, without bending my knees. It is not a bad plan to hold lightish dumb-bells in your hands, when making this latter movement, as the extra weight puts a bigger strain on the abdominal muscles.

The third movement consists of stooping down from full height and touching my toes without bending my knees.

Sparring Practice.

Sparring practice comes next, and here again I venture to think that my method is better than the traditional British style.

Instead of sparring 3 minute rounds, I keep going as fast as I can for as long as my partner will stand it, keeping it up sometimes for as long as 6 minutes at a stretch.

No, it isn't an easy job to find a partner who will go all that racket, and, even if you can, he is hardly likely to do you much good, as he is bound to slow down terribly, and so diminish your speed in consequence.

But how's this for an alternative?

Get three partners, or more, if you can, and the more their styles vary, the better for you.

Say that you are a heavy-weight, and want all the speed you can work up to. In that case, start off with a lightish, quick man, the quickest and trickiest you can get hold of, and set him to dodge and trick and feint you all he knows.

Then, just as you are getting irritated and feeling anxious to get to business, send him back, although he has only been going a couple of minutes or less, and have a good, heavy, quick, fresh man to take your punches and give them back to you.

Keep at him till you have run him off his legs, and have out another quick and fresh man, who will make you travel again, just as you are beginning to feel blown.

Vary this procedure by having all your partners ready gloved in a row, and leave their selection to your trainer. If he knows his business, and also what is best for you, he will send his men up one after the other for a minute or two minutes each, taking care to change them as soon as they begin to slacken down, sometimes sending the heavy man last, so as to practice you in the art of avoiding punishment when you are praying for the bell, and on other occasions sending up a quick hard hitter, who will bustle you hard, just after the big 'un has taken the steam out of you.

If you can keep going well for six minutes at that kind of practice, and especially if your partners are quick and clever and vary much in their styles, you won't stand such a poor chance, even if you are going to box for a **world's** championship.

A Left Hock to Jaw at close range—Right ready for upper cut.

Ball-Punching.

When you have got through your sparring practice, and this should last about 20 minutes or so altogether, you can turn your attention to the punching bag. You can take this opponent in hand for a five round contest, devoting six minutes to a round or to two rounds with a heavy bag to commence with, following up with a similar bout with a medium bag, and winding up the proceedings with a brisk and lively three minutes with a light bag, which you must keep going at top speed.

You won't feel in good condition for such a strain as all this when you first get to work, but it is a system which is worth persevering at, since you are winding yourself up for a harder trial than the whole lot put together, and your best and quickest way of getting into the necessary condition is to train yourself to stick it out, without slackening speed.

One very important point to observe, when ball-punching, is that you should steadily avoid all temptation to do fancy work.

Trick ball-punching is the bane of the boxer. It looks very artistic, no doubt, and, of course, when other men, expert bag punchers, proceed to show you how it is done, you are, especially if you are young at the game, extremely liable to succumb to the temptation to become as clever and smart as they are.

This is a mistake which may easily become fatal. In the States, as you are, perhaps, aware, it is the custom to invite one's lady friends to witness the final stages of one's training.

We have what we call Ladies' Day over there, and it is perhaps, natural for a man to try and study up fancy work in order that he may be able to display his skill and activity on that occasion.

Fight the Bag.

If he does so, however, he must remember that he can only do so at the cost of losing all the value which the punch-ball will be to him as a boxer. For, when training for a fight, he must get into the way of fighting the ball.

By this, I do not mean just standing up to it and sending in drive after drive, just to set it flying backwards and forwards, but that you should look upon it as a shifting, tricky adversary, whom you have to dodge and avoid and punch as he is on the move.

Dance round the ball and practice every variety of punch on it, first from one side and then from the other.

It may not look so pretty as a fancy display, but you will probably find that it calls for quite as much, if not more skill and activity. Skill and activity of a different quality, certainly, but of the brand which will assist you as a boxer. In other words, precisely the kind you want.

Above all, hit the ball hard. Go at it as though you meant to hurt it. The heavy bag will help you somewhat with this ; but it isn't a bad plan to hold a small dumb-bell in each ball-punching glove, to work up your hitting muscles.

I am not a particularly big man myself, and have, in consequence, been occasionally sneered at as a heavy-weight champion, but a good few of my opponents will, no doubt, testify to the fact that I have a very decent punch of my own.

This was first cultivated at hockey and lacrosse, to which two games I owe much of such strength as I possess in my wrists and forearms. Go in for ice-hockey, say, and see how those limbs will be strengthened. Lift the hockey puck on the side of your stick and sky it, or try and " shoot " it along the ice a distance of 50 or 60 yards at about a foot or two off the surface. I can tell you it takes some doing. You have to dig the toes of your

Ball Punching: "A Left Jab."

Ball Punching: Ready with the Right following a Left Jab.

Ball Punching: A Right Punch and ready with Left after shifting round.

Ball Punching: Dance round the Ball and deliver a straight Right.

skates in the ice, give a sharp turn of the wrist as the rubber touches the heel of your stick, and make a long, sharp sweep.

Lacrosse is another game which will pull up your arm muscles. These don't get bunched and hard like a wrestler's or a weight-lifter's, but remain loose and supple, and of the finest quality. Besides which, as you are always on your toes, you will develop your speed and footwork amazingly, and gain enormously in chest development, wind, and stamina.

But I have dropped out of both the lacrosse and hockey worlds lately, and have had to depend on ball-punching to keep my hitting muscles in condition. And the punching bag has done it for me. I have all the punch I have had any use for, and can put them in, one after the other, whenever I want.

In running through this training programme, I am not suggesting that you should carry it out regularly in the order set forth above. This can, of course, be varied according to taste, and it is, perhaps, advisable to change it about pretty frequently. But it should all be run through and not shirked in any way; the work with the ball itself being specially valuable, as it is the finest training for judging distance (if you shift about) that there is, except, of course, the actual sparring practice.

Massage.

The final stage of the day's training work belongs to your trainer. When you have got through the roadwork, the skipping, stomach exercises, shadow fighting, sparring, and ball-punching, and have had another shower bath and rub down, you should lie out on a couch and get your trainer to massage you all over. That is *his* business, and he can only learn it by practical experience, so that I have no advice to give him.

But, in order to show you how important this department is, I may just give you an idea of the operation.

Your trainer will knead you all over from head to foot, pulling, stroking, rubbing, and pinching all the muscles and sinews, in order to take all the stiffness out of them, and to keep them soft and pliable. They must never be allowed to grow hard or knotty, for, if they do, you will find that your arms won't "shoot out" into action just when you want them, and that the other chap's blows will get there first.

It is important that a boxer should guard as little as possible. He doesn't want to have to waste either time or energy over that part of the work.

Besides which the arm so employed can be far more profitably engaged in putting your opponent out of the business. Hence the importance of exercise for developing speedy footwork, to enable you to side-step, slip and avoid, to get out of the way when necessary, and to jump quickly in to close quarters whenever opportunity offers.

The End of the Day.

By the time your trainer has finished with you, you are feeling pretty ready for another meal.

This should come on about 6.30, and should consist of a small steak or chop, with toast and tea. Rhubarb and prunes, or an orange or so, may also be taken.

I am a great believer in tea as a beverage, despite the abuse some doctors and training experts have favoured it with; but, to a certain extent, a man may consult his own tastes in the direction of diet, so long as he sticks to plain, good food, without potatoes or pastry.

He should, of course, avoid all spirits, but there will be no harm in indulging in a glass of beer, now and then, if he feels like one. But it should be taken in strict moderation, at most only once or twice a day.

After dinner, or supper, whichever you care to call it, a pleasant, light conversation, a gentle stroll, perhaps, if the weather is agreeable, and so to bed.

Final Hints for the Heavy-Weight.

A lot of boxers, who are matched at catch-weights, and even other boxers, who have no difficulty in getting down to scale, devote far too much attention, in my opinion, to getting off what they imagine to be superfluous flesh. This, I feel sure, is a mistake, for if a man trains himself extra fine, he is bound to feel tired and to get slow.

Therefore, take all precautions against overdoing it. Go in to the ring a bit heavy, rather than too light; for, you must remember, that loss of weight means loss of strength, as I have more than once discovered in my old middle-weight days.

Above all, never let your work get back on you. If you find it getting monotonous and a drudgery, knock off for a day. You must enjoy your training if it is to do you all the good you want it to do.

Knock off nearly all your gymnastic work during the last two days before the fight itself. Go for a fairly long walk, and just confine your other work to such quick, brisk movements as will give you vim and snap. You want to go into the ring full of fire and eagerness, and so must run no risks of fatigue, weariness, or overstrain.

CHAPTER VI.

On how to Train to Scale, together with advice as to how to recognise and combat Overtraining or Staleness.

When Training to Weight.

Of course, when you have been matched against a man, and will have to weigh in at the ring side, or an hour or two beforehand, at a weight considerably less than you scale before commencing training, you will have to vary the foregoing routine pretty considerably.

On these occasions, the training business is far from being all honey. You scale yourself anxiously every day, and groan sometimes as you think of the pounds still to be taken off.

I have a few melancholy recollections of that period myself, in the days before I fought Marvin Hart and entered the heavy-weight class.

I used often to find any amount of difficulty in getting down to 158 lbs., and on one occasion, when I was getting ready for Twin Sullivan, I had to get rid of 27 lbs., and had only twelve days in which to do it. That was no joke, I can assure you, and it was a relief to me when I knew that those times had gone for good and all.

I cut down my food to two meals a day, and I have always had a decent appetite, even when I have not been training.

I used to rise early, have some rhubarb or an orange, and then go out for my roadwork before breakfast. I sprinted more in those days than I have done since, and got back by 11.30 a.m. to breakfast. This used to consist

Raising the Legs to right angles with the Body by muscular action alone (without bending the Knees).

Sitting up from prone position by exertion of Abdominal and Back Muscles only.

of a couple of eggs, a small chop, toast and tea. After which I rested until about 2 or 3 o'clock, and went hard at it in the gymnasium, following through the routine as stated, and at about 5.30 or 6 had my second meal. This would be a fairly plentiful, plain meal. No potatoes, of course, or anything calculated to make weight, but just plain meat, tomatoes, rhubarb, toast and tea.

After this I would take a short, brisk walk to finish the day.

Even on that fare, I found that I did not come down light enough, and had to starve a bit more, with the result that I went into the ring feeling horribly weak, and lost the decision on points in 20 rounds.

Under the circumstances, I think that I did remarkably well. There wasn't much in it, but I hadn't the strength to finish, and felt badly tired long before I was through.

It was my last experience at " training down," and I made up my mind that I wouldn't try it on again. Big Marvin Hart, about 5 inches taller than myself, and about 2 stones heavier, had beaten Jack Johnson (the coloured heavy-weight) and Jack Root some few months earlier, and had, in consequence, claimed the Championship, which Jeffries had resigned.

He had fixed up a battle with Pat Callahan for January 15th, 1906, but had no objection to taking on a little chap like me on the following 23rd of February.

All the critics laughed at my temerity. Several of them even went so far as to declare the match an iniquity, while the spectators thought that they were just picking up money when they laid 4 to 1 on my opponent's chances.

But I was now under no weight restrictions. I didn't have to bother about the scales, and could go into the ring feeling fit, well, and strong. Hart lasted the 20 rounds, but there was no doubt about the decision, not even Marvin nor any of his friends had any cause or grounds for grumbling, as he himself went to bed after it and stayed there for three full weeks.

I had entered the ranks of the heavy division, and had a claim on the Championship at that, and, as big Jim Jeffries had resigned his title to the winner of the Hart-Root contest, I had, I believe, the best claim of anybody.

Still, I had to battle once or twice more, before I could get this recognised—but that is a story which has nothing to do with training. I have merely quoted the reminiscence as an encouragement to those awkwardly situated boxers, who, having made a reputation at a certain weight, are nervous about risking it by entering among a heavier class, when they are only putting on a few pounds with advancing years. It does not pay to starve and train yourself down below your natural figure. I am aware that the maxim which states that a good big 'un will always beat a good little 'un is full of sense, and has been, and is being, continually justified; yet a 12 stone odd man, who can win battles when he has starved and trained himself down to 11 stone 4 lbs., need have little fear of his success if, at his normal, proper weight, he runs up against even 14 stone men.

If his skill has been great enough to carry him through in spite of his weakness, then, surely, his skill, reinforced by strength and fitness, will enable him to go all the way, even with heavy men.

Besides which, weight isn't all that it is imagined to be. Fitzsimmons, when he walked through all sorts of heavy opponents, never scaled the middle-weight limit, and was, besides, generally giving heavy odds away in years as well.

The worst of training down is that it is such a harrowing, irritating process. A man is far more likely to get stale and to look upon his preparation as a wearisome ceremony, which he is tempted to shirk. He goes into it without enthusiasm, and, consequently, fails to derive the benefit from it which is it's sole *raison d' etre*.

A matter of 7 or 8 lbs. to get off, and plenty of time to do it in, is not such a serious matter with some people, but over that margin it becomes so. Better give the lbs. away and fight at your proper figure. Make your training a pleasure. Select the most cheerful and jolly companions and partners you can find, and pay as much attention to the enlivening of your spirits as you do to the development of your stamina, speed, and hitting power.

Beware of Getting Stale.

Well, every boxer naturally keeps a bright look-out for this bugbear. It is the most serious thing that can happen to him, and unless he can manage to dodge it, he will enter the ring in very little better state than he was before he started training.

The trouble with most boxers is that they don't know how to recognise the signs of approaching staleness, and, in their ignorance, even go so far as to encourage it.

Some wiseacre, in some pre-historic period, conceived the idea that free perspiration was a sure sign that a man wasn't fit, and so most trainers work harder at their men, if they perspire freely, until they get them as dry—and as stale—as a bone.

Now, when I am training hard and find that the pores of my skin are not working freely, I guess at once that I have been overdoing it and am likely to get stale, and I judge that I guess correctly. Anyway, I always knock off all work for one or two days when I get like that, and have a soft, restful time. Then I go back to work, and, if I am again perspiring freely, I consider that I have put my enemy "staleness" out of action.

I don't know whether you will agree with me or not as to the correctness of my judgment in this particular, but you will never be able to persuade me that I am wrong.

One last word on training, and I have done. Remember that you are professional boxers, that you are not in the business for your health alone. So keep a rein on yourself between the contests. Your career, at best, can only be a moderately long one, and that if you go in for cakes and ale after a good win you can only do so at the cost of putting on really superfluous flesh, and of getting badly out of condition. The next time you get "hooked up" or contracted for another bout, you will have to get round again before you can start training proper. To do this properly will mean a long and trying strain. So long and so trying, indeed, that the very word "training" will be hateful to you. You will either shirk it and go into the ring half-trained and unfit, or you will overdo it and enter on your battle stale and used up.

The career of a champion boxer may look nice, soft, and profitable. There are plenty of dollars in it. I won't deny that, but it is not, anyway, as soft as it is cracked up to be.

The Double Shift.

Knocked Out by a Right "Cross."

A Left Head Lead "side-stepped," so as to get into position for a Kidney Punch. Opponent trying to block this with Forearm.

Going into Action "covered up." Left ready for Body.

CHAPTER VII.

Ring Strategy and Tactics.

No matter how well-trained a boxer may be, how hard a punch he may have cultivated, what degree of speed he may have developed, however great the courage, stamina and ordinary boxing science he may possess, he cannot hope to attain championship honours unless he is well up to all the wrinkles of what is commonly known as Ring Craft.

For well-trained, hard-hitting, speedy, brave, skilful, and enduring boxers are to be found in large numbers. A man needs only pluck, determination, and a fairly average intelligence to acquire all these qualities, and no man without these elements can hope to aspire to enter the championship ranks.

The real champion, or he who is destined to become such, must, therefore, fight his way through a whole row of these before he can reach the pinnacle of his ambition, and he will be brought up short, sooner or later, unless he realises that *brains* are the most important and valuable asset he can possess.

A big contest is won by the exercise of hard thought, careful planning, and swift and accurate perception of the right thing to do and the right time to do it.

Infinite patience, also, is frequently indispensable. You may have weighed your opponent up carefully, recognised that he is a most formidable man to have run up against, and yet if you go in and chance your luck, it is not at all improbable that you may regret it.

Do not, on these occasions, fall into the error of supposing that "Fortune always favours the Brave (or, rather, the Reckless)." Bide your time. Draw your man, feint him, worry him. Keep your end up, but run no risks. Put a curb on your impetuosity, and reflect that, though you are getting desperately tired and are anxious to get the business settled, the other man is probably entertaining the same thoughts.

Act on this, and try and make him wearier, more anxious for a speedy termination, and he will, if you do it cleverly, begin to take chances and to make mistakes.

As soon as he does this, your time will begin to arrive. Don't overlook his errors, but get in quick and take advantage of them, and you will reap the reward of your prudence and patience.

Ring Craft, Ring Tactics, Generalship, or whatever you like to call it, is not learnt in a day. Properly speaking, it can only be thoroughly learnt by experience. But, nevertheless, since one can often learn from the experiences of others, some of the following hints may be found useful to you.

First Principles.

The first thing to do when "Time" is called, in any contest, is to take a careful survey of your antagonist. You can spar round him cautiously while you do this, feinting him, threatening attacks and simulating different movements while you are making your observations, and relying on your speed (which I have so often insisted that you should cultivate) to carry you out of harm's way, should he threaten danger.

Above all, take matters easily. Keep cool and confident. Remember that you would not have gone in for this contest unless you were fairly sure of winning, or were crazy (which I don't suppose you to be). The less you fuss and worry the easier and the quicker will victory come to you.

I would also advise you to make no vigorous attack early on. Let your opponent do that, if he feels like it.

Make your Opponent do all the Fighting.

Leave the violent onslaughts to the other man. If he seems as cautious and circumspect as you are yourself, you must try and trick him into a display of his fighting quality. It should not be difficult to do this, supposing you have got yourself fairly well posted as to his methods, general behaviour, and weaknesses; nor should it be difficult to so manage it as to make him show what he is capable of, and yet contrive to keep yourself out of harm's way the while.

In my early days, after having knocked out four or five opponents straight off the reel, I fancied myself no end of a hurricane fighter, and so began to imagine that I had only to go for my man, right and left, all out, to finish him off in next to no time.

The first time I got wise about this was when I ran up against Ed. Sholtreau, whom I had previously knocked out in one round. In I went, and had all the best of a fast and strenuous 5 or 6 early rounds. It was lightning work, and no doubt looked amazingly pretty and spry, but, though I had scored all along the line, I hadn't succeeded in putting my man to sleep, or forced him to quit, and had all but "sewn myself up."

At the end of the sixth round, though I had not been punched to any extent, and had welted the other man pretty severely, I was far and away worse off than he. I had a long tally of points in my favour, but he was still able to come up fairly briskly at the call of Time, while I was feeling as though I wanted horses to pull me out of my chair. I had got to work far too fast, had done all the fighting, and had used up nearly all the wind I possessed in the process. How I managed to last out the remainder of the ten rounds I don't know, but I can tell you that it was only by a big effort. I managed to avoid any serious punishment, but that was all. I got the verdict on points, but I don't think that I deserved it, for I certainly couldn't have gone on any longer, and he would, I think, have lasted another two rounds.

I made much the same mistake later on, when I met with my first defeat (on points) at the hands of Mike Schreck, but after that I had learnt my lesson. I couldn't always expect to knock my opponents out quick and early, so had to calculate on a long drawn out affair, and lay my plans so that I should be on hand and going strong at the finish.

How to Meet a Rusher.

Of course, you will sometimes come up against a man who has no time to spare, and who means to finish things off in double quick time. These gentlemen may look awkward, but, as a matter of fact, they are, barring accidents, dead easy.

I am not referring to the ordinary fighter who sets about business straight away and wants to get to hard fighting immediately. You have to be fairly wary of that kind of opponent, and must cover up, clinch, slip, side-step, and avoid all you know how.

But the reckless, rushing man, who calculates to polish you off in about a couple of rounds, even if he isn't

Taking Punch on top of Head. Going in to close quarters.

Ducking a Left Swing, and sending Right to Body. Ready for a "Clinch."

capable of doing it in a punch, is only dangerous at times, and then only more or less by a fluke.

All you have to do is to keep cool, wait for him, stand firm in front of his rush, and meet him with a well-aimed drive. You can hardly miss him, and he is so intent on settling your hash, that he rarely, if ever, thinks about guarding himself. No matter how good, strong and powerful he may be, his wild rush ought to deliver him into your hands. Still, you must remember that there is a possibility of his getting home, and that, therefore, you must be sure of getting there first.

Bill Squires' Charge.

A striking instance of this may be quoted of my meeting with the Australian champion, Bill Squires.

We had only just faced each other, when he came at me, like a bull at a gate. In a bound he was on me, but my right got there first on the angle of his jaw.

Down he dropped as though he had been poleaxed, and, for just a few seconds, I fancied that the whole business was over.

But in four seconds he was up again, had leapt clear across the ring, and had given me a beauty, right in the mouth. It was one of the worst and hardest blows I have ever received, and for a second or so I was dazed and hardly knew where I was.

But I kept my wits about me, clinched and leant up against him, while I recovered my senses. I wasn't far off being " out," but had no anxiety that he should get acquainted with the fact. So I just cuddled up to him and asked him what he was about. I said that I wanted to know whether he couldn't fight or wouldn't ?

The bluff came off, and I am sure that Squires didn't even guess that he had hit me, while all the reporters stated that I never received a blow at all right through the affair.

He struggled to push me away, and I just leant against him and let him shove, for my senses were fast coming back to me.

We broke in the centre of the ring, and, as he came on at me, just as before, I popped my right over again and dropped him for the second time. He was up in a second, and feeling rather groggy, evidently, but as full of fight as ever. So I just put in as many as I could and as fast as I could make them follow each other. I didn't want to give him an opportunity to recover and give me another like the one I had already received. He dropped his arms. Over came another right to his jaw, and he was down and out in 2 min. 8 sec., one of the shortest, if not the shortest, championship battle on record.

There are one or two morals to this yarn, but the one I wish particularly to impress on you, apart from that which served as a text, is that if you *do* get an awkward, nasty punch, to clinch at once, until you recover, and, above all, to keep the matter dark as well as you are able.

It will be a much bigger score to your opponent if he learns that he *has* scored, and won't help him much if he is ignorant of the fact, and is, consequently, not tempted to take advantage of it.

How to go into Action.

Most professors of boxing try to instill into their pupils the advisability of standing well up and of taking full advantage of every inch which they may possess.

Now, I don't possess many inches, being of a short, stocky build, and yet, as you will possibly have noticed, I generally set about my work in a crouching attitude.

This, according to all rule and tradition as preached by the old-time conservative professors, should rob me of much of the reach which, according also to the same authorities, I could only get full benefit from by standing up as tall as I was able. Well, I haven't a bad reach (7½ inches more than my height), but I haven't found that my crouch has subtracted any from it. I can generally manage to put my fist where I have wanted to put it, even against men who were 3 or 4 inches taller than myself.

I have never found any difficulty in getting in as close as I wanted to get and so have managed either to find their body or to upper-cut them, and I have hardly ever been outreached even when I have wanted to "cross" them. But then I never want to hit "longer" than 18 inches.

Advantages of the Crouching Attitude.

The American Crouch has become an accepted term in ring parlance, and you will admit that Americans know something about the Science of Boxing.

Why, then, should they have generally adopted a pose so totally at variance with all the old traditions?

Well, first of all, by sinking in your chin on your chest, you are covering up fairly securely your most vulnerable point, the jaw.

Then, again, by stooping in this fashion, your body is withdrawn, as far as possible, from the scene of operations, and you don't want any more punches in the stomach than you can help. They are not pleasant in themselves, and, besides, they are not beneficial to your wind.

Drawn in like that, your opponent is not only badly placed to get in a decent drive at your body, and is liable to misjudge his distance should he attempt to get home there, but you yourself are well placed to cover it up with your arms.

As far as your own reach is concerned, you will find that your blows are even more effective when they shoot up from below and are more difficult to parry, as their direction is difficult to judge, while, if you are at all fond of an upper-cut, the crouch will provide you with many useful opportunities.

Hit Short Blows.

In a previous chapter I dealt with the manifold advantages of a short, half-arm blow, one which never travelled more than about 18 inches. The long, straight drive or the big swing look very impressive, no doubt, but they involve an awful waste of energy, which you want to conserve as much as you can, and besides which you are apt to misjudge your distance with them, and to waste a lot of your force on the unoffending air.

The short, quick jab may not present such an imposing appearance, but, in comparison with the old and much belauded method of hitting, it stands in about the same relation as the skilful, rapid foil play of a practised fencer does to the tremendous cleave-you-to-your-midriff slashes of the two-handed sword.

In-Fighting Tactics.

As a rule, it is wisest to reserve all your offensive movements for fighting at close quarters. Then it is generally give and take, and here comes another advantage of the crouch. You are up to your man, with your shoulders rounded and your arms well placed both to cover up securely such small body surface as you may

Fighting the Body in a "Clinch" while your Opponent is holding and helpless.

A Left Hook to the Stomach
(showing the effect of systematic body fighting).

present to him, and also to give him all the digs for which opportunity may occur.

In Amateur Competitions, where the heats are decided in 3 or 4 round bouts, I know that there must be a considerable temptation to regard the head as the most favourable object to attack. Blows landed there *look* awfully effective, and cannot fail to be observed by the judges.

Still, even under these circumstances, I would recommend that the same plan of campaign should be adhered to as in a regular professional 10 or 20 round battle.

A blow at the body is directed at a good, big, almost stationary target. It cannot be avoided with the same ease as can one aimed at the head or face. Then again, the target is nice and soft, and is not calculated to result in injury to one's hands, as will a blow which misses its object and only fetches home on the top or back of the head, such as will frequently be the case when your opponent crouches and covers up.

When you have got home good and hard in the stomach or ribs, and guess that your antagonist is thinking about a clinch to stop your repeating the dose, you can then back away quick and go for the head. This is likely to be open to you better at that time than earlier on.

Should he succeed in clinching, you must look out for an opportunity on the break away.

Sink your own head low at these times, in case he is trying on the same game.

But if you have landed well once or twice in the body and can then get clear quick, you can go for his head pretty quickly and without much fear of reprisals, for he is sure to be too much distressed to be thinking about guarding that portion of his anatomy. He will be more troubled about the places you have just been visiting.

Here comes another advantage of the short jab, for when you have swung or let go a big drive, you are generally slightly overbalanced, have always to pull your arm back, and thus you waste time and give him opportunity to cover up.

Don't *spring* clear, unless there is good cause. His attempt at clinching will fail quite as badly if he only just misses, and you can drive in a good succession of hasty taps, which will be more effective than one big drive, unless, of course, it lands in the right place, when both, of course, are equally efficacious.

Don't Neglect the Body.

For other reasons, this should be your principal object of attack. A blow in the face *seems* to be more effective, but isn't so really, unless, of course, it is a "knock-out," generally difficult to get home, or arrives flush on the nose, and so hampers your opponent, by interfering with his breathing.

Otherwise, head blows rarely get put just where they are wanted to be put, and are recovered from fairly easily during the minute's rest, while a good body blow affects a large surrounding area, and is bound to make an impression.

In a long-drawn out battle you may reckon one good body punch as being worth at least three head punches, while in short bouts their immediately damaging effect will generally leave the head sufficiently open to you to enable you to run up quite a decent tally of points.

Worrying Tactics.

Worry your opponent as much as you can. Cultivate quick, slight movements or tricks with the eyes, hands and feet, which will convey the impression of a sudden, rapid movement, which you do not really carry out.

In many cases, these tactics will cause your opponent to make a big lunge or a rapid jerk or spring backwards or sideways, out of danger, such as will take a lot of steam out of him, without having distressed you in any way.

Always keep on guard, of course, for if he lunges out at you, you must move quickly out of reach, or beat him on time, with your stopping counter or push. You must pay as much attention to his timing and distance judging as to your own.

But with a bull-headed slashing opponent, who is not your equal in science or foot-work, and who depends on his punch to win him the victory, you can safely confine yourself to worrying and feinting him. You need not even trouble to hit him more than once in a round or so.

Keep just out of distance and run through every feint you can think of. Let him come at you as hard and as fast as he can. You can, if you have paid careful attention to the cultivation of your foot-work, just get out of his reach every time. Don't overdo it and make him miss you by yards ; the nearer he gets to you the greater will be his temptation to have another try.

After a while he will lose his head and get wild. Play him up some more of the same game, and when time is called he will go back to his corner, more done up than he would be if you had landed him a whole hurricane of blows. He will have wasted and expended far more effort on missing you than he would have done had he got home every time and received your attentions in return, while you yourself ought to be feeling quite fresh and happy, having gone through little or no exertion yourself, besides which his annoyance and irritation are certain to have told on him.

Change your Tactics.

During the rest he will probably have done some hard thinking, and will, in addition, no doubt have received some very excellent advice from his seconds. You must be prepared for this, and be also prepared to alter your plan of campaign in accordance therewith.

Anticipating the fact that in the next round he will have made up his mind to avoid being fooled again in this fashion, get right into the centre of the ring sharp on the call of time. Then, as he crosses you, turn sharply and get him on the outside circle.

You should be able to judge almost immediately whether he is going to be caught with the same old bait, or whether he has made up his mind to refuse to have any of it. His attitude and first moves will tell you this.

Feint and worry him again, but on a different plan. If he shows signs of being flurried and inclined to anticipate that you are going to repeat your previous dodge, seize the first opportunity to get in and let him know that you are on the premises and mean strict business on this occasion.

As soon as he has got this idea into his head—and he will almost certainly get it there mighty quickly—you can go back to the feinting business, only let it be all indicative of attack this time. He will start slipping you or your threats, and in his condition he will almost certainly do it in earnest.

Well, as he has the outside of the ring to himself, while you are merely turning round in the centre, it follows that he will certainly cover a lot more ground than you, and will, consequently, be tiring himself out some more.

Every time that he gives you a good opening make a really energetic feint, just to keep him lively, and it

Upper cutting a Man who covers up.
(Feint him to protect his face, and then "cut.")

Feinting a Man who "covers up" persistently to get him to fight.

will be politic to go in once or twice in earnest, in order to prevent his forming any certain conviction of your intentions.

Making a Man Beat Himself.

After a while he will get real mad, and will come at you savagely on that account and not because he fancies that you are frightened of him, as he imagined, when you first set about tricking him, and now is the time to address a few remarks which will be calculated to add fuel to his fire.

Go back to the old game, only you can safely keep a little further away now, as his rushes may be dangerous, and he will probably be too annoyed to notice the difference.

Don't get careless, because, owing to his condition, you are able to avoid him so much more easily. Keep cool and calm. You have the game in your hands, and there is no need to run any risk of throwing it away by over-confidence or a desire to display your skill or hitting power.

Stick to the plan I have outlined for you, varying it according to circumstances and on the lines indicated.

It won't be many rounds before he is reeling and staggering, all his wind, confidence and head gone.

Take your time, and when you see that you can do it with absolute safety, step in and put him " out."

It won't be much trouble, as you have " made him beat himself."

How to Fight a Round.

In all cases, make your man do the fighting. Let him come at you, only lure him to come just beyond the distance he meant to find you at. He will be slightly off his balance, and will have lost most of the force of his rush. Get in quickly then, give him what you can find opportunity for, and clinch. That, of course, is when you are not confident enough to fool him.

When in holds, let him do the pushing, keep close up until you are broken away, always taking care to break well clear and well covered up, and repeat the operation.

Reserve your real aggression until about the last half minute. He will (if you have followed my advice) be somewhat distressed, as you have left most of the exertion to him, and you can chalk up your points quickly and comparatively comfortably. If you are not gifted with the capacity to reckon up the flight of time, keep an eye on your seconds, whom you will, of course, have instructed to post you as to the situation.

If you are lucky enough to get in a shrewd punch or two, or have otherwise managed to instil a wholesome respect into your opponent, feint him so as to make him cover up. Then draw clear and laugh at him. The spectators are pretty sure to join in, and this will encourage him to make mistakes and to leave openings. Of course, if a man keeps persistently covered up as Jack Palmer did—well, you will have to use all your brains to find an opening. Provided you are not careless, you won't run any serious risk in looking for it, as a man who covers up like that is pretty sure to entertain a feeling amounting to positive awe and reverence for you, and would not hurt you for worlds.

The Quitter.

Another stamp of opponent occasionally encountered is apt to be embarrassing. This is the man whose main idea would appear to be the avoidance of anything resembling a genuine contest, and who confines his efforts to getting out of your way. One has to be very careful with these gentry, for they are almost invariably very skilful *boxers* and past masters in the wiles of Ring Craft. They must necessarily be so, or otherwise, with their distaste for fighting, they could never have attained the reputation and position which would qualify them to oppose anyone who was bent on climbing the championship ladder.

My readers will possibly remember the tale of the negotiations which preceded my two last fights with Jack O'Brien, especially the second one. Well, as soon as the referee had declared that " all bets were off," Master Jack became suddenly aware that his schemes had fallen through, and that if he was to emerge victorious from the ring, he could only hope to do so by virtue of his proving himself the better fighting man of the two.

Evidently, he failed to fancy himself in this capacity. I may be wrong, but I am entirely wedded to the impression that his whole attention was bent on preserving as wide a separation from me as the size of the ring would allow.

One would have thought that he would at least have seized the opportunity to test the correctness (or otherwise) of the published opinions of my boxing ability or lack of it. On the contrary, he seemed to be altogether indifferent to any discovery of this quality in me, and to be curious rather as to my abilities as a pedestrian, sprint or long distance runner.

Be that as it may, I have a high respect for his qualities in that department. He set me a hot pace, and it took me all my time to catch up with him. Now and then I managed to get him in a corner or against the ropes, but he always slipped out and set off again, and the chase was resumed.

He was very smart in keeping his head out of the way, so that I could only visit his body, and I had, of course, to exhibit a certain amount of caution. It was clear that he was not only a sprinter, but was also no slouch at long distances; so that if I distressed myself in the pursuit, or grew annoyed or careless, he might get an opportunity to get home a chance blow to my jaw, and so save himself any more running.

Gradually it became clear that he would do his best to refrain from giving me any opportunity of knocking him out, so all I could do was to follow him round and chalk up as many points as possible, whenever I could corner him. Things had been much the same on the occasion of our first meeting, although he had stood up and fought one or two rounds at Los Angeles the first time, and there was also the annoying recollection that the battle had then been declared a draw.

But I had to keep cool and refrain from being worried either by this remembrance or by the fear of having all my labours similarly thrown away now. He wasn't doing any scoring that I could see, except as a clever dodger and fast runner. Surely they would remember that this had been styled a *fight* for the "Championship of the World," and not a running match, and would give their verdict accordingly.

Well, as all the world knows, they did so decide, and I was accordingly qualified to defend the title against all comers. Jack, however, has not yet quit the ring for the cinder path, though honestly I can't help thinking that he would reap many honours there.

When you get Knocked Down.

This, of course, happens to us all at different times. No man can guarantee that he will always succeed in

Finishing a Man whom you have made "beat himself."

The Right Way to Take the Count.

dodging a nasty one on the jaw. It isn't pleasant to get one of these punches, but it is right down foolish to make a mistake when it happens.

Remember always that you have full 10 seconds' rest, which you can take on those occasions, and you may as well have those 10 seconds.

Don't be in a hurry to jump up and rush at your man. Get up slowly on to one knee, facing your opponent, and stay so till the count of 9. You have then a whole second more in which to rise to your feet.

Any punch which sends you down is bound to make you a bit dizzy, and it is surely wise to let as much of the dizziness evaporate as you can before you get to business again.

CHAPTER VIII.

The Complete Second.

The labours of the seconds in a big ring contest are most frequently their own reward. That is to say, that, while all the glory and honour of a won battle will go to the victorious principal, a good half of these should frequently be bestowed upon his astute advisers and caretakers, who will almost certainly be accorded quite their share of the blame should their man be defeated.

Almost always a man's trainer accompanies his charge into the ring, and on such occasions likes to assume the position of chief second or adviser, although, strange to say, he is rarely qualified for this office, the duties of trainer and second being by no means akin.

It is, in fact, difficult to say how a second's qualifications are to be discovered. Experience in training, skill in boxing go for nothing, most of the historical seconds having but poor ring records of their own. A chief second, in fact, need not necessarily ever have been a boxer at all. But he must have been a keen spectator at numerous contests, must be a good judge of character, an accurate and quick observer, and, above all, a wary and highly suspicious individual. He must also be even-tempered and indifferent to the display of jealous feelings in others. These last he will always have to put up with, since his man's trainer, being human, will be unable to conceal his resentment at having to drop into the ruck as soon as the second appears on the scene.

For, on the day of the fight itself, it is this gentleman who takes full charge, not only of the principal himself, but of the bottles, sponges, alcohol, or other liniment, towels, fans, ice, and all other apparata which will be in use at the ring side. None of these must leave his possession for a moment. I would not suggest that there are people so devoid of principle as to seek to dope or interfere in any way with any of these appliances, but it is just as well to remove temptation out of their way.

Arrived at the ring side, he delivers his luggage to the respective wardens, of whom the bottle holder, apparently the most insignificant, has by no means the least arduous functions. There is no necessity for him to enter the ropes; in fact, he is best outside, where his implements are; and, although he has to pass the bottle over to the towelling or fanning second, and the embrocation to the trainer, who is best suited to the duties of masseur, and may possibly be called upon to apply the ice block to his principal's back and shoulders as well, yet must he take due care that none of these pass beyond range of his vision until they are no longer needed.

Inside the ropes is the masseur, the chief toweller, and the adviser (or second *par excellence*). The last-mentioned alone should have power of speech, the others being mere automata.

I trust "Gunner" Moir will not mind my saying so, but I would venture to suggest that he would have done better had the friends in his corner realised the advantage of adhering to this last-mentioned rule.

Better one man's advice, even though it be bad advice, than half-a-dozen people all talking at once and all talking differently. No two men are likely to notice the same thing in the same way, or to draw the same conclusions therefrom. The principal can think for himself, and accept or reject his adviser's hints and instructions as he will, but if he has four or five advisers he is liable to be uncertain as to whether he has been doing any thinking at all, or even as to whether he is capable of thought.

If he isn't much of a general and has confidence in his adviser, it is best for him to quit planning and to confine himself to obeying orders.

How a good Second may win a fight for his Principal.

No boxer, however clever he may be, can afford to disregard the advice and hints of his second. The latter is the "looker-on," who sees most of the game. He is best placed to judge when and where his principal may have succeeded in landing a telling blow, for, as previously instanced, a boxer may succeed in getting home as forcibly as Squires managed to get home on my mouth, and yet be totally unaware of his good fortune.

Then, again, certain punches may have a far greater effect than the man who has delivered them has any opportunity of discovering. They may have been delivered just prior to clinching, when the other man closed and held, in order to disguise the effect which had been produced.

I have seen a man who, otherwise a good staunch fighter, was always liable to partial collapse if hit severely in the lower right ribs. Being aware of this, he always covered up this vulnerable point very carefully, but, as often happened, he did get thumped there now and again, when his right arm was temporarily elsewhere.

On these occasions he invariably endeavoured to clinch, partly to disguise the fact that he was suffering

Squires. The Great Burns-Squires Fight. Tommy Burns.
Jim Jeffries
(*Referee*).

from the effects of the blow and partly to remain in holds, until these effects had to some extent passed away. He was a remarkably clever boxer and won many battles before his vulnerability became widely known.

So clever was he, however, that the first man to get well posted on the subject was a well-known second, who happened to be acting for several opponents of his, and who also happened to be in their corners on two or three consecutive occasions.

On the first of these his man had been having considerably the worst of the exchanges, and in the seventh round looked as though he would never last out. More by accident than design, however, he twice got home in the lower right ribs with a half-arm left jab. He noticed nothing very especial himself, but his second, who was eagerly looking for anything that might possibly give him a hint as to how the situation might be saved, noticed on each occasion that his man's opponent drew in his breath as if with pain and immediately went into a "clinch," from which he was in no hurry to break away.

Here might be a possible chance, so he decided on persuading his man to risk everything on it.

As soon as the gong went and he had his man sitting in the chair, he got at him. "Now," said he, "you're pretty well behind on points, but you can win easily. As soon as you come together, get to close quarters. Chance everything; feint him for a right at the head and just show him your left jaw uncovered. Keep the tail of your eye on his right, and as it comes up, cuddle your chin down and drive for the lower ribs with your left. It's got to be a short punch, for you must get in one or two before he can clinch. If it comes off, try it again. Don't try and push him away when he clinches, because you don't want to puff yourself any more, but wait till you are separated by the referee. Don't forget you've got to chance things; the right lower ribs are what you're going for."

There was, of course, any amount of risk in this advice, for it *might* not have been quite such a vulnerable point as it appeared to be. The second's principal had had a fair welting and was going weak, so that his punch would not be so effective as it might have been, and then the other man might reach the jaw before it went into cover or before his own man's left got home.

Nevertheless, the risk was taken, and it came off. Three times did the back-marker reach the spot in the eighth round, and before those three minutes had elapsed the other chap was so busy guarding his weak point from any further visitation, that he got knocked down with a left on the jaw. He came up weak and tottery for the ninth time; the second advised his man to feint at the ribs and then hit at the head, and again the advice was the right dope. Early in the tenth round the second's generalship was fully justified.

He was now fairly posted as to the other man's weakness, so he followed him up and got into the opposite corner whenever he could. One more trial, and he was aware that he had stumbled on no chance weakness. He kept the knowledge to himself as long as he could, but it soon leaked out, and the other man had to retire from the ring.

This, of course, was an exceptional case, but I have quoted it *in extenso* in order to illustrate the value of a good second. In many cases he is probably better acquainted with the good and weak points of the opposition than his principal has had any chance of becoming. For the ideal second naturally makes a point of studying every fighter whom he sees in action. Every boxer has naturally a favourite punch, or a favourite duck, parry

A. F. BETTINSON, Esq.
(*Manager of the National Sporting Club.*)

or slip, just as he has concealed somewhere about his anatomy some spot in which he has a strong aversion to be punched.

He is, as a rule, too busy fighting himself to notice which of these moves he relies on most readily. These will be brought into operation almost instinctively, while, on the other hand, he can only become acquainted with his weak spot by repeated visitations. He may not suffer any abnormal quantity of these, and when any do come he may perhaps put down the consequent spasm as being due solely to the extra force which his opponent has employed. His adversaries, again, are generally far too busily occupied to make an analytical examination of him. So that both strong and weak points are liable to remain undiscovered until some extra skilful opposing second happens to spot them.

I may have weak and strong points of my own, but if I have I have never seen them advertised, nor have I heard mention of them.

Am I acquainted with them myself? Well, is it likely that I should proclaim the facts aloud?

The second, again, must nurse his own man. He should be posted as to his weaknesses, and, above all things, prevent him throwing away his chances by sailing recklessly into action against a crafty opponent, who has every intention of staying the limit.

He should also be able to judge, and to judge correctly, when the time comes, for his man to " burn his boats," by going in to win right away, chancing a " knock-out," for the simple reason that it is now or never with him. He must also be able to judge the right line of tactics, which his man should pursue to enable him to pull round again after he has had a lot of gruel, that is, supposing him to be a man who is gifted with great recuperative powers. Sparring out and dancing out of the way won't do it if carried to excess. This will only tire him just a shade less than a regular mix-up. A steady, skilful retreat, backing-up, well covered, " milling on the retreat," as it used to be called, is the right policy at such a time.

His man must go as steadily as possible, saving himself all necessary exertion, trying to tempt his opponent to rush him, and meeting such rushes steadily with a straight left. Care must be taken to avoid being pinned into the ropes, and here the steering voice of the second will prove of almost inestimable value.

Another very valuable quality for a second to possess is an instinctive appreciation of the flight of time, for he will have to serve somewhat in the capacity of a clock-face to his principal. It is not a bad plan to arrange a code of signals by which the second can communicate the passing of the minutes without, at the same time, similarly apprising the opposition. It is very useful for a boxer to know when the last half, minute has been entered upon.

Spare your Principal all Avoidable Exertion.

Have the chair back into the ring the instant that the gong goes. Meet your man as he comes into his corner, and seat him as gently as possible in the shortest possible space of time. Get his limbs loose and muscles relaxed for the rubbing down without the slightest semblance of delay. Set the towels or fans working instantly, but see that they are waving clear. Don't shut the air off him. Make him draw long full breaths not only while in his corner, but while boxing, whenever he gets a chance, such as when he or his opponent is breaking ground.

On no account allow him to talk. You have to do that. His duty is to listen. Whether he follows the advice given, is, of course, his look-out, but at least let him hear all that you have to offer. Let this be clear and concise. Don't get excited or flurried yourself in any way, for if you do you will only flurry and excite your charge. Tell a man off (the bottle-holder, say, since he is the least occupied) to watch the opposition corner closely and to immediately report to *you* any crooked thing which he may observe.

At the call of time, you and the towel-flapper should raise your man gently by the arms and lift him bodily (but without any jerk) on to his feet. It is but a slight exertion which you have spared him, but it is the little points which count in a boxing contest, and even the slightest exertion is a very big little point. For the same reason it is not a bad plan to advise your man to work over to his own corner towards the end of each round, so that he has but to turn round and sit down when the gong goes. Similarly, he need not be in any undue hurry to leave his chair at the call of time. Four or five seconds saved each round in these two operations will tot up considerably in a long fight.

CHAPTER IX.

On Fouls.

In all my series of battles, I have never either won or lost a fight on a foul. I am not going to say that I have never been fouled, or have never had a foul attempted on me, but that none of these were ever noticed by the referee as being of sufficient importance to call for the disqualification of my opponent.

Nevertheless, one has always to be very wary of any such attempts. So many are allowed to pass unnoticed, and so many others are censured, which were neither fouls according to the rules, nor being legal fouls, were anything but accidental. Now, in professional matches at least, a boxer is generally allowed to hit in a clinch, as long as he has one hand free, to hit with, and yet I have seen men cautioned, if not disqualified, for so doing. I have also seen a man disqualified for apparently persisting in holding his opponent, when, as a matter of fact, his opponent was persistently holding him.

This is an artful trick, to which some shady boxers resort, especially if the referee is at all weak.

They will bore into a man quickly and trap one of his arms either between one of their own arms and their side, or round their neck, clipping it there by pulling on his crooked elbow. They will then apparently tug back a little as though to get free, and will be rewarded for their craftiness by hearing the referee order the other man to desist from holding.

This foul, and most others, are far more likely to be credited to the guilty party in America than they are in England.

I have praised the National Sporting Club for many good and sufficient reasons, but there is one point in which I venture to suggest, that they might improve not only their own methods, but that of Boxing generally in the Old Country.

So many English referees now adopt the American method of officiating inside the ropes, that surely the Club might see its way to follow the example.

Then *the* foul blow. The shady class of boxers who descend to the use of this, generally contrive to deliver it when their backs are turned to the referee. Now, if he is seated outside the ring, at a distance of a few feet from the ropes, it is extremely difficult for him to detect whether this was really a foul blow, intended as such, or merely one which was accidentally forced down by a parry—even supposing him to notice the exact delivery itself.

Fouls, with the knee or elbow, are also far more easily detected when the referee is close at hand, and, when one considers how serious these can be, I am surprised that every precaution is not taken to guard against their employment.

Butting is another artful foul, which is very difficult to detect, and here your sole hope lies in the referee. He may not see the " butt," in which case your only remedy is an appeal. Your seconds will, of course, appeal likewise; but the mischief will, of course, often have been done. No matter whether the referee notices the incident or fails to do so, you must avoid losing your temper, for to lose this means losing your head, and, in the long run, very probably the fight itself as well.

CHAPTER X.

The Boxer's Disease, which is too often the cause of his downfall.

Why is it that so many promising boxing careers are so often suddenly cut short, and that a man who seemed well on the high road to fame and affluence should so suddenly find himself back in the ruck, losing class and caste, and heading straight for poverty and trouble?

These instances, and they are fairly numerous, are generally seized upon as evidence of the debasing influences which beset the Profession; and are held up as warnings to aspirants in order to prevent such from entering upon a course which, as shown by the examples selected, can only end in want and misery

Yet similarly promising careers in other lines of life have the same melancholy ending. In each case, the cause is identical. The sufferers have been afflicted with one of the most dire diseases to which humanity is subject, but to which Boxers are, perhaps, more prone than other people. This disease is known as " Swelled Head."

A Case in Point.

When I picked up young George Memsic, I guessed that I had got hold of some " good goods," had found a man who, with a little coaching, ought to become light-weight champion.

He only weighed 133 lb., which is the American lightweight limit, and bar a tendency to try and mop up his adversaries straightaway, had every needful qualification for a champion at his weight.

When I took him in hand, he received the nickname of " Jimmy Burns," and as long as I was in his corner to see that he did not allow his impetuosity to carry him away, he did nothing to cast discredit on his new appellation.

He was badly down on his luck when I first took him in hand, despite a fairly lengthy and a really good record, but he had not possessed the business ability to get himself good hauls out of the purses he had fought for, and he had steadily spent his money as fast as he earned it.

Well, I took him up and taught him Ring Craft. I seconded him and made him " back up," that is, draw away from the other fellows, leaving them to do the fighting and to make openings for him. He was broke and almost starving, so I paid his fare to California, where he beat the Montana Kid in 10 rounds, knocked out Charlie Neary in 2 rounds, beat Fred Sheer in 3 rounds, Charlie Neary again in 10, Johnny (" Cyclone ") Thompson in 20—this was by sheer Ring Craft. Then he knocked out the Montana Kid in 7 rounds, and had very little the worst of a 20-round battle with the great Joe Gans. The first of these fights was on September 14th, 1906, and the last September 27th, 1907.

I wanted him to come over to England with me, but no, he had plenty of money now, fancied himself a fair terror, and didn't want any more of my assistance. So ; and I hear he has now done in most of his money and has been beaten by Unholz, a lad we had as his sparring partner, and one whom he could beat whenever he wanted to.

No, Jimmy must have had a bad attack of "swelled head." He probably thought that Unholz was "dead easy," treated him cheap, and paid the penalty, as have many better men before him.

That's the worst disease likely to attack a boxer. No amount of inoculation seems to render them immune from "swollen head." A most dangerous malady, which not only makes them lose fights, but lures them on to waste their money as well.

Look at all the good boys I have known who have succumbed to its attacks, besides poor Jimmy. There have been Young Corbett, Terry McGovern, the great John L. Sullivan himself, the peerless George Dixon, Kid Lavigne, Pedlar Palmer, Peter Jackson, Jack Dempsey, and scores of others. They all did well in their time and made thousands of dollars, which they racketed and dissipated away, paying the first penalties in disease and defeat, and the final ones in poverty, destitution, and too frequently a pauper's grave.

There are two coon songs, very popular over the water, which we boxers hear often enough, but the moral of which few of us take to heart. The first is—

"When you ain't got no money, you needn't come around"; and the other—

"Put your hand on your pocket-book and loudly cry, 'Here's my friend!'"

There's wisdom for your use in both these. Jim Jeffries, Tommy Ryan, Jack O'Brien, Ben Jordan, Joe Bowker, Jimmy Britt, Tom Sharkey, and Battling Nelson have seen it, and can all of them walk past a poor-house without seeing visions.

As for Tommy Burns—well, they say "that he keeps his money in his pocket so long, that he has to send it to the laundry every week to get the creases taken out."

CHAPTER XI.

Some Facts and Explanations.

I was born on June 17th, 1881, at Hanover, Ontario, my father being French and my mother German. My parents moved to Chesley, Ontario, when I was still very young, and it was with the Chesley team that I first started playing Lacrosse.

By the time I was twelve years old I was reckoned good enough for the town team, although the next youngest player was nineteen or twenty.

I stuck chiefly to Lacrosse for several years, and was a member of the Galt team which won the Championship of Western Ontario in 1898; but went in for football, skating, swimming, diving, base-ball, basket-ball, and hockey as well. I won the third prize in the Ontario Skating Championship Tournament, and generally ran up pretty well at swimming meetings, etc.

I became a member of the Detroit Athletic Club, and went over to see a boxing night there. One of the entrants didn't turn up, so I volunteered, just for the fun of the thing, to take his place. As it happened, I won my bout in the fifth round. The prize was a money one, but it did not occur to me till some one told me that I had entered the professional ranks by winning this fight.

Well, as the milk was now spilt, I thought I would see whether there were any dollars in the business, and entered for all the fights which the club gave during the next two years. There were eight of these, and I won them all, so that I got plenty of chances to go further afield.

One of my stiffest fights in Detroit was with Ben O'Grady, of Buffalo. He was a pretty tough customer, and had a trick of trying to frighten his opponents at the outset. As soon as he got into the ring he started off to his seconds with—" Shall I kill him ? " " Which round shall I knock him out in ? " and so on ; and when we met in the middle of the ring he started off to me, ' Well, you're here, are you ? "

" Yes," I said, " I'm here." " Well," he replied, " you won't be here in a little while."

I knocked him down twice in the first round, and pointed out that I was still there. He knocked me off my feet in the second round, but I got up and kept going. In the third, I put him out, and it was four days before he came round. The police took charge of me during those four days, and even escorted me to the hospital when I wanted to see how O'Grady was going on. It was a nervy four days for me ; but, fortunately, O'Grady pulled round all right, and I was glad to find that he was doing well when I met him in Buffalo two years ago.

The hardest go I ever had was with Billy Woods, at Seattle, on September 16th, 1904. It went 15 rounds, and was called a draw. It doesn't matter now, but I felt sore over that decision, far more sore in mind than Billy had made me in body, though, perhaps, not so sore as I had made him.

In all, I have fought over fifty battles, the chief of which have been as follows :—

In 1900, knocked out Fred Thornton in 5 rounds, at Detroit ; knocked him out again in 5 rounds at Delray. In 1901, knocked out Billy Walsh in 5 rounds, Archie Steele in 2, Billy Walsh, again, in 6, and Ed. Sholtreau in 1, all at Detroit, where I also beat Sholtreau 3 weeks later in 10 rounds, and later on Dick Smith at Mount Clemens, also in 10 rounds. In 1902, I knocked out Dick Smith at Mount Clemens in 9 rounds ; Reddy Phillips, at Lansing, in 9 ; and Jack O'Donnell in 8, at Butler, Ind. ; I also beat Tom McCune, in Detroit, in 10 rounds, but lost on points to Mike Shreck, also in 10 rounds, at Detroit, on November 29th, 1902. In 1903, I beat Jim O'Brien in 10 rounds at Delray, and knocked out Dick Smith in 2, Reddy Phillips in 3, Harry Peppers in 2, Tom McCune in 7 rounds (all at Detroit), Jimmy Duggan in 9 at Houghton, Jack Hammond in 3, and Jack Butler in 2 rounds at Sault Ste Marie, and Jack O'Donnell at Evanston in 11 rounds. I also drew with Billy Moore in 10 rounds at Houghton on October 25th. In 1904, I knocked out Ben O'Grady, at Detroit, in 3 rounds ; Geo. Shrosbee, at Chicago, in 5 ; Joe Wardinski, at Salt Lake City, in 1 ; Cyclone Kelly, at Tacoma, in 4 ; and Indian Joe, at Ballard, Washington, in 6. I fought 3 draws that year : Mike Shreck, 6 rounds, at Milwaukee ; Tony Caponi, 6 rounds, at Chicago ; and Billy Woods, 15 rounds, at Seattle ; lost a 6 round affair on points with Jack O'Brien, at Milwaukee, and beat Tony Caponi on points at Chicago, in 6 rounds, less than 3 weeks after my drawn fight with him.

In 1905, I drew with Twin J. Sullivan, March 7th, in 20 rounds, at Tacoma ; beat Dave Barry, May 3rd, also 20 rounds, at Tacoma ; drew twice with Hugo Kelly, in 10 and 20 rounds, at Detroit and Los Angeles, on June 7th and July 28th ; knocked out Dave Barry, in the 20th round, at San Francisco, on August 31st ; and lost on points to Twin J. Sullivan, at Los Angeles, on October 17th. N.B.—This was my last attempt to get down to 158 lbs.

In 1906, I beat Marvin Hart for the Heavy-Weight Championship of the World, in 20 rounds, at Los Angeles, on February 28th; knocked out both Jim O'Brien and Jim Walker, 1 round each, both in the same ring, at San Diego, on March 28th; knocked out Jim Flynn, at Los Angeles, in 15 rounds, October 2nd; and fought a 20 round draw with Philadelphia Jack O'Brien (for the Championship), at Los Angeles, on November 28th. In 1907, beat Joe Grim, at Philadelphia, in 3 rounds, on January 10th; beat Phil. Jack O'Brien, at Los Angeles, 20 rounds, May 8th (World's Championship); knocked out Bill Squires in 1 round (also for the title), July 4th, at Colma, Cal.; and, finally, also Gunner Moir, in 10 rounds, at the N.S.C., London, England, on December 2nd.

I have lost three battles in all, and only three. What is more, they have all been "on points." My first defeat, as I have said, was at the hands of Mike Shreck, before I got wise. I beat myself there. The second was when Jack O'Brien was adjudged the winner of a 6 round contest, and I had only two days in which to train for that.

My third and last defeat was by Jack Twin Sullivan, when I had to get down to weight, and went very weak in consequence. Still, I lasted the 20 rounds, and there wasn't so very much in it. That was my last middle-weight battle.

I don't know whether you have noticed it, but I am rather proud of the fact, that I am the first American Champion of the World who can claim to have beaten the Australian and English Champions, as well as those of my own country (for, although born a Canadian, I am an American citizen, and have never sought to disguise the fact). Jim Jeffries certainly beat Peter Jackson, but then Peter was the ghost of his old self at the time.

Eugene Corri

(Referee—Burns-Moir Fight)

"Gunner" Moir.
(*Champion of England.*)

I know that no Australian or English champion went running after Jim, but that doesn't alter the fact that he didn't have their scalps to hang at his belt.

Excuse this crow of mine, but if I don't make it, other people may forget to make it for me ; and, since I intend to defend my title against all comers, I don't see why I shouldn't have that intention recognised at its full value.

I have been styled a third-rate champion, and may, possibly, be such ; but, if that be a fact, then all the other boxers knocking about just now must be only fourth-raters, and I wouldn't like to class them as such, despite all that the critics have to say. It's curious, but the *de*-merits of my rivals are only discovered after I have done with them.

The Correct Version of the incident at the National Sporting Club.

In my preface I gave my reasons for wishing to give the facts concerning a certain rather absurd incident, which has received a far bigger advertisement than it needed. This was the little scene in the ring just before my fight with Moir, which I have explained once or twice to various pressmen, who have, nevertheless, continued to harp on it in the old strain, taking as their text the wildly improbable version served up to the American Press.

These are the facts. The first thing I was told when I landed in England, a total stranger to everyone and everything, was that you had a law whereby a man need not pay a bet if he didn't want to. Could plead the Gaming Act, and so get out. I had my own money at stake, and, naturally, didn't want to risk it for nothing. So I mentioned what I had been told to the officials of the National Sporting Club, and it was suggested, more,

I think, with a view to be friendly to me than for any other reason, that if both the side-bets were deposited with Mr. Blacklock and handed by him to the referee before the fight, to be given to the winner at its conclusion, before awarding his decision, there could be no possibility of trouble. Naturally, I had no objection to make to this, and, equally naturally, as I think, I just enquired whether this had been done when I got into the ring.

Mr. Bettinson thanked me for reminding him, and handed the stakes over to Mr. Corri, and there the matter might have terminated, had not a few excitable people seemed to have imagined that I was worrying about the purse. As a matter of fact, I wasn't in the least disturbed about either the stakes or the purse. The N.S.C. is a club of honourable men, and I did not need to be assured of this.

I did not, as has been alleged, seek to explain matters to anybody at the time. Everyone who needed any explanation, or who was entitled to such, was perfectly satisfied the same evening, and expressed regret that, through ignorance, they should in any way have misconstrued what occurred.

In conclusion, I may say that, while as sportsmen and Britishers they would naturally have preferred to see the Gunner victorious, yet it would have been impossible for them to have given me heartier applause or more genuine congratulations than they accorded me, nor would I ever wish to fight before a fairer and more sportsmanlike crowd.

You Britishers are men, white men, and as good sportsmen as there are in the world. All I hope is that you will allow that I, too, have tried throughout to be as white as you are.

www.ingramcontent.com/pod-product-compliance
Lightning Source LLC
Chambersburg PA
CBHW070152100426
42743CB00013B/2886